vybnf VAL
613 WELLN

Wellnes
334100

1

D1561865

At Issue

| Wellness Culture

Other Books in the At Issue Series

At Issue

| Wellness Culture

Sabine Cherenfant, Book Editor

GREENHAVEN
PUBLISHING

Published in 2022 by Greenhaven Publishing, LLC
353 3rd Avenue, Suite 255, New York, NY 10010

Cover image: Rawpixel.com/Shutterstock

Library of Congress Cataloging-in-Publication Data

Names: Cherenfant, Sabine, editor.
Title: Wellness culture / Sabine Cherenfant, book editor.
Description: First edition. | New York : Greenhaven Publishing, 2022. |
   Series: At issue | Includes bibliographical references and index. |
   Audience: Ages 15+ | Audience: Grades 10–12 | Summary: "Anthology of
   diverse viewpoints exploring how lifestyle, business, and health
   intersect to create today's wellness culture"— Provided by publisher.
Identifiers: LCCN 2021001108 | ISBN 9781534508125 (library binding) | ISBN
   9781534508118 (paperback) | ISBN 9781534508132 (ebook)
Subjects: LCSH: Health—Juvenile literature. | Nutrition—Juvenile
   literature. | Exercise—Juvenile literature. | Lifestyles—Juvenile
   literature.
Classification: LCC RA776.5 .W457 2022 | DDC 613—dc23
LC record available at https://lccn.loc.gov/2021001108

Manufactured in the United States of America

Website: http://greenhavenpublishing.com

Contents

Introduction

The University of California defines wellness as "an active process of becoming aware of and making choices toward a healthy and fulfilling life."[1] The choices do not relate only to physical activities. Wellness also includes different dimensions like emotional well-being and social well-being. Nevertheless, wellness has lost a lot of its positive appeal because of how quickly the culture could turn toxic. In recent years, the wellness culture has gained in popularity and has become an industry, further invigorating itself into mainstream culture. Whether or not this is a good development is the biggest question—and potential issue—facing the industry. How do we balance it out? This industry has also seen itself attached to diet culture and to a race to be thin because thinness is, oftentimes, equated to being healthy and well. Lastly, what does the wellness culture teach us about social class, race, and gender? Those are all questions worth considering when evaluating the issues surrounding wellness culture.

As noted by Ryan Corte of IntroWellness, there exists no set or universally agreed-upon definition for the word *wellness*. Merriam-Webster, Cambridge Dictionary, and Oxford Dictionaries, just to name a few, each has its own definition of the word.[2] Yet, all of the definitions hint to a conscious pursuit to achieving a sense of well-being. Evidently, achieving that stage involves an awareness of eating habits, physical activities, and mental and emotional health.[2] Eastern New Mexico University identifies six branches of wellness. They are emotional wellness, environmental wellness, intellectual wellness, spiritual wellness, social wellness, and physical wellness.[3] They involve being in control of one's emotions, building self-esteem, respecting the environment, nurturing one's critical thinking and world knowledge, finding purpose in one's life, developing strong relationships with others, and keeping an active lifestyle.[3]

But, because wellness culture focuses so much on healthy behaviors, it can degenerate into an obsession and a dependence on subjects like foods and physical exercise. As a result, wellness culture is often tied to eating disorders like anorexia nervosa and bulimia. This is also because wellness is tied to the diet culture. Being thin is celebrated, and this, in turn, can trigger those eating disorders. According to the Mayo Clinic website, although it is impossible to determine what officially triggers anorexia nervosa, one of the most common eating disorders, one of its potential causes is cultural because in many societies people's value is based on their body.[4] Moreover, body image is something that affects mostly women and teenage girls, and those groups are primarily the ones who suffer from the aforementioned eating disorders.

Bethany Ao of the *Philadelphia Inquirer* describes another eating disorder, not yet listed in the *Diagnostic and Statistical Manual of Mental Disorders* (*DSM-5*), named orthorexia nervosa, which consists of obsessing over eating healthy to the point that it becomes unhealthy.[5] In this case, even though wellness promotes keeping track of what is put in the body, if not done properly, it can backfire and promote guilt and unhappiness. Rosie Spinks of *Quartz* writes that less than 1% of Americans suffer from orthorexia, and the disorder is often disregarded as healthy eating obsessions. Moreover, the percentage jumps to 86 when focusing on wellness professionals and workers.[6] Spinks also points out that one of the reasons why it isn't recognized as part of the *DSM-5* is because there are no agreed-upon symptoms associated with the disease.[6]

This obsession with healthy eating is also magnified on social media. A quick look at Instagram reveals a plethora of pages dedicated to helping users reach a health goal. The benefit of social media is that it provides access. Users are able to follow fitness gurus, meditation experts, and nutritionists, where they can participate in workout challenges and receive wellness advice. Knowledge and help that was once reserved for face-to-face, expensive interactions can now be accessed online. Nevertheless, the pages are often managed by influencers with lean bodies and comfortable lifestyles that do not reflect the lives of most of their followers. This makes wellness culture aspirational at best. Marisa Meltzer of *The Cut* writes that wellness culture is also about luxury and wealth. It is as much of a wealth staple as a Hermes or Chanel bag.[7] She further adds, "We once called all of this pampering. Now we justify it as self-care, necessary time spent for our health—physical, spiritual, emotional."[7] This idea of self-care in itself is embedded in high living because it is not accessible. It requires a lot of spending and time to reach that ultimate wellness. It is not something the average person can afford.

Wellness, however, is very important in work culture as people struggle to find a work/life balance. In an article in *Forbes* magazine, Michael Blanding writes that one of the driving forces of health care costs in the United States is workplace stress, making up approximately $190 billion in expenses.[8] Factors like long hours and harsh corporate demands can lead to health problems like diabetes, hypertension, and heart disease. Additionally, the majority of our time is spent at work.[8] Evidently, people who are in toxic work environments, who experience taxing demands from their managers and who work in fields with a high mental toll are more likely to develop health problems.

This is where wellness comes into play. Finding activities outside of work is important to the well-being of professionals. Activities that tackle emotional, social, and physical well-being can help in alleviating stress and balancing out life. Companies, as well, have a good reason to develop a wellness culture in their workspace as this helps establish a better work environment with happy and productive employees. *Forbes* contributor Alan Kohll states that by building a culture of wellness at work, companies are telling their employees that they are valued; cultivating the mental and physical health of employees by sharing important information on nutrition and encouraging them to prioritize their health helps companies keep productivity high.[9] Indeed, people perform better when they are in a better state of mind.

Obesity is another health problem that the wellness industry aims to address. This may have started with an emphasis on exercise and changed eating habits, but it also addresses trauma and other emotional problems that people often struggle with. The goal is a well-rounded journey to betterment. Indeed, there has been a shift in the messages being delivered to the public. Body positivity images and advocacy are taking over the narrative. This, too, in a way, is part of wellness culture as it pushes the boundary on the definition of emotional wellness, which deals with self-image. Instagram accounts promoting lean, sculpted bodies are countered by opposing accounts urging the public to accept and appreciate their body as it is. Celebrities and activists like Lizzo and Jessamyn Stanley are redefining what wellness and self-image mean. This also helps in the fight to empower women in general. Nevertheless, popular fitness trainer Jillian Michaels was criticized for voicing her opinions about singer Lizzo's weight. Michaels believes the singer's body should not be celebrated as it undermines the fight against health conditions sparked by obesity. Is her argument pertinent? Or is there a way for those different movements to coexist without undermining the other's effort?

Whether or not wellness culture is leading a positive movement depends on a person's viewpoint. By definition, it promotes a balanced life and personal growth, whether by pushing one's body, mind, or spirit. There are a lot of controversies surrounding it, however. First and foremost, it has become an industry partly led by social media influencers advertising a lifestyle that is not attainable by most people. Moreover, at its worst, wellness culture seems to encourage eating disorders by focusing so much on physical activities and healthy eating. At its best, it tackles the national obesity crisis and the importance of alleviating corporate stress. Is wellness culture a positive movement or an advertising agent for a consumer industry? In *At Issue: Wellness Culture*, viewpoints presented by diverse authorities explore the many facets of this question.

Notes

1. "Student Health and Counseling Services," The University of California, Davis Campus, n.d. https://shcs.ucdavis.edu/wellness/what-is-wellness.
2. Ryan Corte, "What Is Wellness and Why Is It Important?" IntroWellness, January 5, 2020. https://introwellness.com/health/what-is-wellness/.
3. "Types of Wellness," Eastern New Mexico University, n.d. https://my.enmu.edu/web /wellness/wellness-types.
4. "Anorexia Nervosa," Mayo Clinic, n.d. https://www.mayoclinic.org/diseases-conditions /anorexia-nervosa/symptoms-causes/syc-20353591.
5. Bethany Ao, "How Instagram Creates 'The Perfect Storm' for Orthorexia, an Obsession with Healthy Eating," *Philadelphia Inquirer*. https://www.inquirer.com/health /wellness/orthorexia-eating-disorder-social-media-20200309.html.
6. Rosie Spinks, "Is Wellness Culture Creating a New Kind of Eating Disorder?" *Quartz*, August 23, 2017. https://qz.com/1059682/is-wellness-culture-creating-a-new -kind-of-eating-disorder/.
7. Marisa Meltzer, "Why Wellness Is the New Way to Look, Feel, and Act Rich," *The Cut*, July 18, 2016. https://www.thecut.com/swellness/2016/07/why-wellness-is-the -new-luxury-lifestyle-status-symbol.html.
8. Michael Blanding, "Workplace Stress Responsible for Up to $190B in Annual US Healthcare Costs," *Forbes*, January 26, 2015. https://www.forbes.com/sites /hbsworkingknowledge/2015/01/26/workplace-stress-responsible-for-up-to -190-billion-in-annual-u-s-heathcare-costs/#1ca22aa2235a.
9. Alan Kohll, "How You Can Nurture a Culture of Wellness," April 6, 2017. https://www .forbes.com/sites/alankohll/2017/04/06/how-you-can-nurture-a-culture-of -wellness/#5e0edb621525.

1

The Idea Behind Wellness Is Not New

Global Wellness Institute

Global Wellness Institute is a nonprofit organization that aims to educate the public and private sectors about preventive health and wellness.

Wellness has a very long history. The modern concept took shape as early as the 1950s, but the practice itself dates back to 3000 BCE. Different civilizations have their own form of wellness pursuit. This can be seen in ancient Hindu, Chinese, and Greek traditions. Nevertheless, according to what is written in the Oxford English Dictionary, the word wellness *was first introduced in the 1650s. Over the years, wellness became more than a lifestyle for the few; its benefits were being acknowledged by the medical industry and the government. It also became a key in fighting increasing health care costs and the obesity epidemic.*

Wellness is a modern word with ancient roots. As a modern concept, wellness has gained currency since the 1950s, 1960s and 1970s, when the writings and leadership of an informal network of physicians and thinkers in the United States largely shaped the way we conceptualize and talk about wellness today.

The origins of wellness, however, are far older—even ancient. Aspects of the wellness concept are firmly rooted in several intellectual, religious, and medical movements in the United States and Europe in the 19th century. The tenets of wellness can also

"History of Wellness," Global Wellness Institute, LLC. Reprinted by permission.

be traced to the ancient civilizations of Greece, Rome and Asia, whose historical traditions have indelibly influenced the modern wellness movement.

Ancient Wellness

3,000–1,500 BC: Ayurveda—originated as an oral tradition, later recorded in the Vedas, four sacred Hindu texts. A holistic system that strives to create harmony between body, mind and spirit, Ayurvedic regimens are tailored to each person's unique constitution (their nutritional, exercise, social interaction and hygiene needs)—with the goal of maintaining a balance that prevents illness. Yoga and meditation are critical to the tradition, and are, of course, increasingly practiced worldwide.

3,000–2,000 BC: Traditional Chinese Medicine (TCM), one of the world's oldest systems of medicine, develops. Influenced by Taoism and Buddhism, TCM applies a holistic perspective to achieving health and wellbeing, by cultivating harmony in one's life. Approaches that evolved out of TCM, such as acupuncture, herbal medicine, qi gong and tai chi, have become core, modern wellness—and even Western medical—approaches.

500 BC: Ancient Greek physician Hippocrates is possibly the first physician to focus on preventing sickness instead of simply treating disease, and also argued that disease is a product of diet, lifestyle and environmental factors.

50 BC: Ancient Roman medicine emphasized disease prevention, adopting the Greek belief that illness was a product of diet and lifestyle. Ancient Rome's highly developed public health system (with its extensive system of aqueducts, sewers and public baths) helped prevent the spreading of germs and maintained a healthier population.

19th Century Intellectual & Medical Movements

In the 19th century new intellectual movements, spiritual philosophies and medical practices proliferated in the United States and Europe. A number of alternative healthcare methods that focus on self-healing, holistic approaches, and preventive care—including homeopathy, osteopathy, chiropractic, and naturopathy—were founded during this era and gained widespread popularity in both Europe and the United States. Other new philosophies were more spiritually oriented (such as the "mind-cure movements," including New Thought and Christian Science) and were instrumental in propagating the modern idea that a primary source of physical health is one's mental and spiritual state of being.

While some of the beliefs espoused by the thinkers behind these movements have been discredited, or seem "wacky" today, these movements did popularize ideas about regaining or maintaining one's health through diet, exercise and other lifestyle measures. The philosophies embodied in these 19th century systems—that a healthy body is a product of a healthy mind and spirit—are now considered precursors to the current, thriving wellness and self-help movements. In addition, although these approaches fell out of favor with the rise of modern, evidence-based medicine in the mid-20th century, several of them are now regaining favor within the mainstream medical community and the general public.

1650s: The use of the word "wellness" in the English language—meaning the opposite of "illness" or the "state of being well or in good health"—dates to the 1650s, according to the Oxford English Dictionary. The earliest published reference is from the 1654 diary entry of Sir Archibald Johnston: "I … blessed God … for my daughter's wealnesse." The first citation with modern spelling is from a 1655 letter from Dorothy Osborne to her husband, Sir William Temple: "You … never send me any of the new phrases of the town… Pray what is meant by wellness and unwellness?"

1790s: German physician Christian Hahneman develops Homeopathy, a system that uses natural substances to promote the body's self-healing response.

1860s: German priest Sebastian Kneipp promotes his "Kneipp Cure," combining hydrotherapy with herbalism, exercise and nutrition. The New Thought movement also emerges, around Phineas Quimby's theories of mentally-aided healing.

1870s: Mary Baker Eddy founds spiritual-healing-based Christian Science. Andrew Taylor Still develops Osteopathy, a holistic approach grounded in manipulating muscles and joints. **1880s**: Swiss physician Maximilian Bircher-Benner pioneers nutritional research, advocating a balanced diet of fruits and vegetables. The YMCA launches as one of the world's first wellness organizations, with its principle of developing mind, body and spirit.

1890s: Daniel David Palmer develops Chiropractic, focused on the body's structure and functioning.

1900s: John Harvey Kellogg (director of the Battle Creek, Michigan Sanitorium) espouses a healthy diet, exercise, fresh air, hydotherapy and "learning to stay well." Naturopathy, focused on the body's ability to heal itself through dietary and lifestyle change, herbs, massage and joint manipulation, also spreads to the US from Europe. Austrian philosopher Rudolf Steiner develops the spiritual movement of anthrosophy and the holistic system of anthrosophical medicine. Another Austrian, F.X. Mayr, develops "Mayr Therapy," a detoxification and dietary modification program.

1910: The Carnegie Foundation's Flexner Report, a critique of North America's medical education system for lack of standards and scientific rigor, questions the validity of all forms of medicine other than biomedicine, resulting in most alternative systems (homeopathy, naturopathy, etc.) being dropped from mainstream medical education, and setting the stage for our modern disease-oriented, evidence-based medicine.

20th Century: Wellness Spreads and Get Serious

Our modern use of the word "wellness" dates to the 1950s and a seminal—but little known—work by physician Halbert L. Dunn, called *High-Level Wellness* (published1961). Although Dunn's work received little attention initially, his ideas were later embraced in the 1970s by an informal network of individuals in the US, including Dr. John Travis, Don Ardell, Dr. Bill Hettler, and others. These "fathers of the wellness movement" created their own comprehensive models of wellness, developed new wellness assessment tools, and wrote and spoke actively on the concept. Travis, Ardell, Hettler and their associates were responsible for creating the world's first wellness center, developing the first university campus wellness center, and establishing the National Wellness Institute and National Wellness Conference in the US.

From 1980-2000, the wellness movement begins to gain momentum, and get taken more seriously by the medical, academic and corporate worlds. For instance, Hettler's National Wellness Institute caught the attention of Tom Dickey and Rodney Friedman, who then established the monthly *Berkeley Wellness Letter* (1984), designed to compete with the *Harvard Medical School Health Letter*, pointedly using "wellness" in the title as contrast. This influential academic publication presented evidence-based articles on wellness approaches, while also debunking numerous health fads. More medical establishment validation: in 1991 the US National Center for Complementary and Alternative Medicine (NCCAM) was established, as part of the government-funded National Institutes of Health.

More government-sponsored programs to promote healthier lifestyles launched in US cities/states. The modern concept of wellness also spread to Europe, where the German Wellness Association (Deutscher Wellness Verband, DWV) and the European Wellness Union (Europäischen Wellness Union, EWU) were founded in 1990.

At the latter end of the 20th century, many corporations began developing workplace wellness programs. The fitness and spa industries globally experienced rapid growth. And an ever-growing line-up of celebrities and self-help experts started bringing wellness concepts to a mainstream audience. However, despite all these disparate developments, this momentum had not yet coalesced under the formal banner of a "wellness industry."

Several Key Moments

1950s: J. I. Rodale, one of the first advocates for organic farming in the US, launches *Prevention* magazine, a pioneering publication in promoting alternative/preventative health.

1950s–1960s: Physician Halbert L. Dunn presents his idea of "high level wellness" in 29 lectures, and then publishes these ideas in his influential book by the same title.

1970s: Dr. John Travis, influenced by Dunn, opens the world's first wellness center in California, and publishes a 12-dimension wellness assessment tool, *The Wellness Inventory* (1975) and *The Wellness Workbook* (1977)—the latter both in use today. Don Ardell publishes *High Level Wellness: An Alternative to Doctors, Drugs and Disease* (1977, referencing Dunn's work). The University of Wisconsin-Stevens Point (UWSP), drawing on Travis' materials, establishes the first university campus wellness center, with campus wellness centers spreading throughout the US in the 80s. In '77-'78, Dr. Bill Hettler of UWSP organizes the National Wellness Institute and first National Wellness Conference.

1980s–2000s: Workplace wellness programs, the fitness and spa industries, and celebrity wellness and self-help experts take off—bringing wellness into the mainstream.

21st Century: The Tipping Point

A 2010 *New York Times* article on the word/concept of wellness noted that when Dan Rather did a *60 Minutes* segment on the topic in 1979, he intoned, "Wellness, there's a word you don't hear everyday." But "…more than three decades later," the *NYT* noted, "wellness is, in fact, a word that Americans might hear every day…" And it's more than Americans paying attention to wellness. In the 21st century, the global wellness movement and market reached a dramatic tipping point: fitness, diet, healthy living and wellbeing concepts and offerings have proliferated wildly—and a concept of wellness is transforming every industry from food and beverage to travel.

By 2014, more than half of global employers were using health promotion strategies, while a third have invested in full-blown wellness programs (Bucks Consultants report). Medical and self-help experts who promote wellness (such as Drs. Mehmet Oz, Deepak Chopra and Andrew Weil) became household names. "Wellness," essentially, entered the collective world psyche and vocabulary and is firmly entrenched with the media and an increasing number of medical institutions and governments.

Healthcare Costs Drive the Shift to Wellness

With a chronic disease and obesity crisis raging worldwide in this century, leading to unsustainable healthcare costs, the traditional medical establishment and more governments are shifting the focus to prevention and wellness. For instance, if, in the 1990s, most academic medical centers had an adversarial stance toward complementary medicine, now many of the most elite institutions in the world feature Integrative Medicine departments.

For example, in 1999, in the US, eight medical institutions (including Harvard and Stanford) convened at a historic conference, the Consortium of Academic Health Centers for Integrative Medicine. Today, membership spans 60 esteemed institutions such as Yale, Harvard and the Mayo Clinic. In Europe, respected, large institutions, such as Charité University Medical Center (Berlin), the Karolinska Institute (Stockholm), and the Royal London Hospital, have large Integrative Medicine centers. And again, in the US, fast-growing federal and foundation research funds (close to $250 million annually just from NCCAM and the National Cancer Institute) are dedicated to research on complementary medicine, wellness and prevention. The American Board of Physician Specialties, which awards board certification to medical doctors, announced that, in 2014, it would begin accrediting doctors in Integrative Medicine.

Wellness Milestones

2008: Bhutan embraced democracy and includes Gross National Happiness within their constitution, saying, "The State shall strive to promote those conditions that will enable the pursuit of Gross National Happiness." His Majesty Jigme Singye Wangchuck, the Fourth King of Bhutan, who questioned the premise that Gross Domestic Product (GDP) alone could deliver happiness and wellbeing to society, conceived the term in the 1970s. In 2011, The UN General Assembly passed "Resolution Happiness: towards a holistic approach to development," urging member nations to follow the example of Bhutan and measure happiness and wellbeing and calling happiness a "fundamental human goal."

2011–2018: With obesity and diabetes skyrocketing, from 2011–2018, there was a flurry of new laws taxing soda/sugary drinks in nations across the world. A few examples with dates of legislation: Finland 2011, Hungary 2011, France 2012, Mexico 2014, Chile 2014, UK 2016–2018, UAE 2017, Portugal 2017, Saudi Arabia 2017, Sri Lanka 2017, Ireland 2018, and South Africa 2018. Norway bumped up sugar taxes in 2018, and US cities, such as Berkeley, CA; Oakland, CA; Boulder, CO; Philadelphia, PA; and Seattle, WA, all passed new soda tax laws.

2012: On April 1, 2012, the first *World Happiness Report* was released, now an annual publication of the United Nations Sustainable Development Solutions Network. The groundbreaking report used data from the Gallup World Poll and measured the state of happiness in 155 nations, the key causes of happiness and misery, and policy implications for countries worldwide.

2014: The Global Wellness Institute (GWI) launched and released research finding that the global wellness industry was a $3.4 trillion market or 3.4 times larger than the worldwide pharmaceutical industry. The GWI research also benchmarked the 10 sectors comprising the global wellness market: Beauty & Anti-Aging ($1.03 trillion), Healthy Eating/Nutrition/Weight Loss ($574 billion), Fitness & Mind-Body ($446 billion), Wellness Tourism ($494 billion), Preventative/Personalized

Health ($433 billion), Complementary/Alternative Medicine ($187 billion), Wellness Lifestyle Real Estate ($100 billion), Spa Industry ($94 billion), Thermal/Mineral Springs ($50 billion), and Workplace Wellness ($41 billion).

2017: In October, the GWI, along with Dr. Richard H. Carmona, 17th Surgeon General of the United States, announced *The Wellness Moonshot: A World Free of Preventable Disease*; a call to action to eradicate chronic, avoidable disease worldwide by uniting the health and wellness industries.

2018: In January, the Global Wellness Institute released *Build Well to Live Well*, the first in-depth research to analyze the $134 billion global wellness real estate and communities sector. The report found that real estate and communities that intentionally put people's health at the center of design, creation and redevelopment are the next frontiers in real estate.

On June 9, the sixth-annual Global Wellness Day, which is considered the first day dedicated to living well, took place. It was celebrated in more than 100 countries at 5,000 different locations.

In October, the GWI released an updated *Global Wellness Economy Monitor*, finding that the world wellness economy grew from a $3.7 trillion market in 2015 to $4.2 trillion in 2017—growing nearly twice the rate of the global economy (3.6 percent annually). The report stated that wellness expenditures are now more than half as large as total global health expenditures ($7.3 trillion), and the wellness industry represents 5.3 percent of global economic output.

In November, the GWI released an updated *Global Wellness Tourism Economy Monitor*, finding that wellness tourism grew from a $563 billion market in 2015 to $639 billion in 2017, or 6.5 percent annually, more than twice as fast as tourism overall (3.2 percent). And in the report, wellness tourism is forecast to grow even faster through 2022 (7.5 percent yearly) to reach $919 billion.

2019: In January, *The Wellness Moonshot™ Calendar: A Year of Inspiration* was launched in support of *The Wellness Moonshot™: A World Free of Preventable Disease*.

2

Wellness Culture Must Understand and Consider Multiculturalism

National Wellness Institute

The National Wellness Institute is an organization that provides professional development opportunities and helps wellness practitioners advance in their career.

For wellness to be a comprehensive practice, an understanding of cultural competency must take priority. Diversity and wellness go hand in hand because, as the author writes, "wellness has different meanings for different populations." It is important for wellness practitioners to have a better understanding of diverse communities to better work effectively. The National Wellness Institute created the Multicultural Wellness Wheel to help health and wellness practitioners meet this goal. It consists of three pillars: personal and family wellness, community wellness, and worksite wellness.

The Mission of the National Wellness Institute (NWI) Multicultural Competency Committee is to support NWI with increasing inclusiveness by advancing multicultural competency within wellness best practices, and to assist with the development of knowledge, awareness, and skills to deliver equitable and culturally appropriate programs and services for wellness practitioners, organizations, underserved populations, and communities.

"Multicultural Competency in Wellness," National Wellness Institute. Reprinted with permission from the National Wellness Institute, Inc., NationalWellness.org.

The goals of the Multicultural Competency Committee include:

- Foster inclusiveness to advance multicultural competency within comprehensive wellness best practices and service delivery.
- Systematically integrate diversity and multicultural competency within the operations and programmatic structure of NWI.
- Develop initiatives, programs and continuing education focused on diversity and wellness to address differences related to: race, ethnicity, class, gender, age, country of origin, culture, political, religious and other affiliations, language, sexual orientation, as well as physical and cognitive abilities and other human differences.

Wellness is considered to be an active process of becoming aware of and learning to make choices (healthy choices) that lead toward a longer and more successful existence.

Wellness has different meanings for different populations. The first step towards an effective wellness program is understanding what it means to your audience.

Multicultural Wellness Wheel

The Multicultural Wellness Wheel is designed to support wellness practitioners and related stakeholders in broadening their outlook as it relates to the concepts of wellness and well-being, and to support the recognition of the interlocking systems displayed within the wheel. This concept map addresses applied multicultural competency and the needs and goals of individuals, families, and workplaces. It also provides a guide for the development of well communities and civic infrastructures.

The Multicultural Wellness Wheel focuses on three pillars for optimal and lifelong well-being.

Personal & Family Wellness
Integral Wellness

- NWI's Six Dimensions of Wellness
- Healthy daily habits—self-efficacy

Integrative Medicine

- Integral healing-oriented medicine
- Conventional medicine
- Alternative medicine

Community Wellness

Supporting underserved communities and minimizing healthcare disparities via the following approaches:

- Upstream: Policies, incentives & regulations
- Midstream: Collaborations, resources and skills
- Downstream: Grassroots initiatives

Worksite Wellness

Worksite Diversity Initiatives

- Cultural sensitivity
- Value-driven organizational culture

Work/life Balance Components

- Awareness of the importance of a balanced life
- Time & energy management
- Tools to help prioritize

How Can Wellness and Healthcare Practitioners Develop and Apply Multicultural Competency?

By becoming aware of one's own personal assumptions about human behavior, values, bias, stereotypes, and personal limitations. Practitioners learn who they are as "cultural beings" and how cultural socialization has shaped their worldview and their ability to work effectively with culturally diverse populations.

A culturally skilled practitioner is one who actively attempts to understand the worldview of their culturally different clients without negative judgments, and shows respect and appreciation for human differences.

A culturally skilled practitioner is mindful of actively developing and practicing culturally appropriate intervention strategies and working appropriately within diverse communities.

Serves as a Tool for Sustained Engagement…

The Multicultural Wellness Wheel serves as a tool for sustained engagement and personal reflection, supports dialogue and discussions, and assists practitioners with individual, family, workplace, and community wellness initiatives related to their unique communities of practice.

The wheel fosters the building of healthy relationships across cultural differences within diverse communities of practice.

Measuring Worksite Wellness Programs by Multicultural Competencies Standards

If your worksite wellness program were to be measured against multicultural competency standards, would it meet, exceed, or fall short of those standards? As you will see, ensuring that your program considers the attributes and demographics that make up culture is mandated by a number of federal laws, renders a greater return on your investment, and serves the public good. When I speak of multicultural competency as it relates to worksite wellness, I am looking at the competency of those who design and implement the program as well as the program's overall effectiveness in serving people of different cultures. Multicultural competency requires the individuals designing or implementing the program to:

1. Be aware of their own cultural worldviews
2. Possess knowledge of different cultural practices and worldviews
3. Examine their own attitudes toward cultural differences
4. Explore the attitudes of those they serve toward cultural differences

5. Have the interpersonal skills necessary to communicate and effectively interact with people across cultures

Many people confuse "diversity" with "multicultural competency." They mistakenly use the terms interchangeably. While diversity is a good starting point, diversity does not equal multicultural competency. Nor do you achieve diversity by varying your team considering race alone. Cultural competency encompasses more than race. Culture includes such things as religion, gender, socioeconomic status, geographic location, language, sexual orientation, and education. Having a diverse group of people at the table is an excellent way to learn about other cultures; it is a way to begin to meet the second requirement on the list above (to possess knowledge of different cultural practices and worldviews).

Multicultural competency is a skill that must be learned. The answer as to whether your team has multicultural competency skills will largely turn on the answer to the following question: has your team had multicultural competency training? If the answer is no, then your team is probably lacking some element of multicultural competency.

To determine if your program measures up, I say the proof is in the pudding. It's not just about your intentions; it's also about results. Evaluate your program to see its effectiveness across cultural lines and whether it is in compliance with laws designed to eliminate discrimination and promote inclusion in wellness programs.

Why Should Worksite Wellness Programs Focus on Multicultural Competency?

Why should you care if your program measures up by Multicultural Competency standards? Simply put, because the law says you must and because you should!

You should be concerned about the effectiveness of your wellness program across cultures for the good of it—the social good, as a good business practice, and because programs that lack multicultural competency simply "ain't good."

Social Good

The CDC predicts that worksite wellness programs will become part of a national public health strategy to address an increase in chronic diseases that could cost the US healthcare system an estimated $4.2 trillion annually by 2023. Chronic diseases linked to health disparities are connected to, among other things, variances in cultural health norms, healthcare literacy, and provider delivery systems, as well as the provider's culture and multicultural competency. Worksite wellness programs can only achieve a notable impact on national public health by reducing chronic diseases if those programs effectively reach groups that are most impacted by chronic disease. Multicultural competency is a core ingredient in reaching those suffering with chronic diseases.

Smart Business Decision

According to the March 2011 Thomson Reuters Workforce Wellness Index, unhealthy behaviors of employees in the US cost employers an average of $670 per employee annually. The Society for Human Resource Management (SHRM) states that there is evidence indicating that healthier lifestyles among employees are a plus for employers, because "[e]mployees who pursue healthful behaviors have fewer illnesses and injuries than other workers, and they recover from illnesses and injuries faster."[1] Wellness programs that encourage healthy behavior can therefore reduce sick days and workplace injuries.

Racial and ethnic health disparities add another layer to the correlation of employee health and business productivity. Many employers are generally unaware of racial and ethnic health disparities as a business issue.[2] It is important to recognize that many chronic diseases related to health disparities, such as hypertension, diabetes, cancer, cardiovascular disease, and obesity, greatly effect productivity and absenteeism. It follows that reducing or better managing of chronic diseases improves productivity and absenteeism. Since ethnic minorities and the poor have higher incidences of chronic diseases, reaching these populations (which is achieved with culturally competent programs and coaches) is critical to improving productivity numbers and reducing absentee numbers.

Lastly, studies have shown that effective wellness programs reduce the cost of insurance. Therefore, not only is there social good in positively impacting people's wellbeing and reducing the stress on the US healthcare system, there is a good business case for effective wellness programs that speak to a cross section of the population. A multiculturally competent wellness program will only serve to increase productivity while further reducing insurance cost and other expenses related to absenteeism. The business case is simply that it will improve the bottom line.

Standardized Programs Don't Work

Racial and ethnic minorities comprise approximately 1/3 of the US population and are projected to equal 54% by 2050.[3] Plus, as described above the workforce today is diverse in ways that go beyond race and ethnicity (religion, age, sexual orientation, creed, geographic, etc.). Differences affect health norms, access to care, environmental health factors, desired providers, and wellness journey preference. A program that fails to factor in culture will fail to meet the preferences and needs of large segments of the workforce, likely resulting in less program participation or less than optimum results.

Worksite wellness programs must comply with numerous federal laws requiring that employers recognize disparities as well as genetics and physical and mental limitations when designing programs to avoid discriminatory behavior and impact.

Patient Protection and Affordable Care Act

The Patient Protection and Affordable Care Act promotes and funds prevention and wellness in the interest of public health. The Affordable Care Act explicitly sets out to reduce health disparities and improve the health of racially and ethnically diverse populations.

The Act was passed by Congress and then signed into law by President Obama on March 23, 2010. It is comprised of the Affordable Health Care for America Act, the Patient Protection Act, and the healthcare-related sections of the Health Care and Education Reconciliation Act and the Student Aid and Fiscal Responsibility Act. It also amends several other federal laws, such as the Health Insurance Portability and Accountability Act of 1996 (HIPAA), the Employee Retirement Income Security Act (ERISA) of 1974, and the Health and Public Services Act. Additionally, it reauthorizes the Indian Health Care Improvement Act (IHCIA).

The Act prohibits discrimination in wellness programs that are group health plans. It is very prescriptive as to standards and requirements that must be met to avoid discrimination in these wellness programs.

The Age Discrimination in Employment Act of 1967 (ADEA)
The Age Discrimination in Employment Act of 1967 protects people who are 40 or older from discrimination because of their ages with respect to any term, condition, or privilege of employment, including hiring, firing, promotion, layoff, compensation, benefits, job assignments, and training.

An example of a practice that could cause issues with ADEA is if the wellness program has a mandatory program that requires employees to meet a certain health standard which does not consider the age of the employee.

Americans with Disabilities Act (ADA) and the Rehabilitation Act of 1973
Title I of the ADA is a federal civil rights law that prohibits an employer from discriminating against an individual with a disability in connection with, among other things, employee compensation and benefits. Title I of the ADA also generally restricts employers from obtaining medical information from applicants and employees. Additionally, Title I of the ADA prohibits

employers from denying employees access to wellness programs on the basis of disability and requires employers to provide reasonable accommodations (adjustments or modifications) that allow employees with disabilities to participate in wellness programs and also to keep any medical information gathered as part of the wellness program confidential.

Note: The ADA does not, however, prohibit employers from inquiring about employees' health or doing medical examinations as part of a voluntary employee health program as defined by the ADA. For guidance on designing a wellness program that is ADA compliant, read "Are You Up-to-Date on ADA and Wellness Programs Compliance?—EEOC's Final Rule on Employer Wellness Programs and the Americans with Disabilities Act."

The Rehabilitation Act of 1973 makes it illegal to discriminate against a qualified person with a disability in federal agencies, in programs that receive federal financial assistance, or in any federal employment, including the employment practices of federal contractors. It also requires that employers covered by the Act make reasonably accommodations for the known physical or mental limitations of an otherwise qualified individual with a disability unless doing so would impose an undue hardship on the operation of the employer's business.

An example of how a program could violate the ADA or the Rehabilitation Act is when an employer has a program that rewards employees for taking so many steps a day or walking a certain number of miles a week. An employee with a disability that limits his or her ability to walk could not be participate and therefore cannot earn an award in the program (the additional compensation). To remain in good standing, the program would need to provide alternative methods for the disabled employees to earn the additional compensation.

Title VII of the Civil Rights Act of 1964 (Title VII)

Title VII makes it illegal to discriminate against someone on the basis of race, color, religion, national origin, or sex. It generally applies to employers with 15 or more employees, including federal, state, and local governments. It considers disparate impacts. Disparate impact is when your practices or program adversely affect one group of people with a protected characteristic more than another although rules are neutral. Certain races are at risk of drastically higher rates of high blood pressure, high cholesterol, and diabetes. Tethering premium savings to what the program has defined as a "healthy level" of these measurements could be seen as discriminatory under Title VII.

The Act also requires that employers reasonably accommodate applicants' and employees' sincerely held religious practices, unless doing so would impose an undue hardship on the operation of the employer's business. A violation on religious grounds could arise if an employer requires employees to submit to a health screening to qualify for savings on their premiums and an employee refuses to submit to the screening based on religious beliefs.

The Genetic Information Nondiscrimination Act of 2008 (GINA)

GINA is a federal law that forbids discrimination on the basis of genetic information in health insurance and any aspect of employment. It has two parts, Title I and Title II. Title I prohibits discrimination based on genetic information by health insurers and group health plans. Title II prohibits discrimination based on genetic information in employment. Genetic information includes information about an individual's genetic tests and the genetic tests of an individual's family members, as well as information about any disease, disorder, or condition of an individual's family members (i.e. an individual's family medical history). For guidance on designing a wellness program that is GINA compliant, read "Are You Up-to-Date on GINA and Wellness Programs Compliance?— EEOC's Final Rule on Employer Wellness Programs and GINA."

Health Insurance Portability and
Accountability Act of 1996 (HIPAA)

The Health Insurance Portability and Accountability Act (HIPAA) was first enacted to address the problem of the uninsured. HIPAA includes provisions that limit exclusions for preexisting conditions under group health plans. It prohibits group health plans and health insurance issuers from discriminating against enrollees and beneficiaries with respect to eligibility, benefits, and premiums based on a health factor, with some limited exceptions.

A wellness program that is a part of an employer-based health plan could face problems under HIPAA if the wellness program is not "reasonably designed" to promote health or prevent disease, or if the full reward is not available to all similarly situated individuals.

State Laws

Be sure to look at your state laws as well the federal laws mentioned about. For example, some state laws prohibit an employer from penalizing an employee from engaging in lawful conduct outside of work[4] including smoking,[5] drinking, and eating fast food. Restrictions related to smoking may not comply with those state regulations.

Endnotes

1. https://www.shrm.org/ResourcesAndTools/hr-topics/benefits/Pages/DecliningHealth.aspx
2. Employer Survey on Racial and Ethnic Disparities: Final Results. The National Business Group on Health. July 30, 20083
3. US Census Bureau. (August 14, 2008). "An older and more diverse nation by midcentury." Retrieved May 13, 2014, from https://www.census.gov/newsroom/releases/archives/population/cb08-123.html)
4. Examples of states that protect employees from being fired for legal off-duty activity include California, Colorado, New York, North Carolina, and North Dakota.
5. There are a host of states that specifically protect tobacco use, including Connecticut, the District of Columbia, Illinois, Indiana, Kentucky, Louisiana, Maine, Minnesota, Mississippi, Missouri, Montana, Nevada, New Hampshire, New Jersey, New Mexico, Oklahoma, Oregon, Rhode Island, South Carolina, South Dakota, Tennessee, Virginia, West Virginia, Wisconsin, and Wyoming.

3

Diet Should Focus on Health and Culture, Not Food Trends

Karena Yan

Karena Yan is a senior associate at the diaTribe Foundation. She recently graduated from Washington University with a bachelor's degree in biology and global health and environment.

The health and wellness culture has an ethnocentrism problem. Food that gets promoted as healthy may not reflect food that is enjoyed and consumed in different cultures. Nevertheless, food consumed elsewhere can be as healthy as food consumed in Western culture. For example, chia seed is touted as healthy but is not part of Chinese cuisine. However, bitter melon is, and this vegetable helps in reducing blood sugar. To combat chronic diseases like diabetes, dieticians need to help patients find diets that fit their food culture.

Cultural sensitivity and relevancy are key to making nutrition advice accessible to everyone.

"What is a chia seed?"

My mom asked me, perplexed by a recipe for chia seed pudding that she came across online. For my Chinese immigrant parents, chia seed is not part of their vocabulary, let alone their pantry. No matter how trendy it is or how many times it's labeled a "super food," there is little chance that my parents, and perhaps many other immigrants, would know how to integrate it into their cooking.

"How Can We Make Mainstream Trends of Health and Wellness More Inclusive of Other Cultures?" by Karena Yan, The diaTribe Foundation, December 2, 2019. Reprinted by permission.

Their resistance is not because they're disinterested in health and well-being—the dissonance comes from the fact that our East Asian nutritious foods simply look different from the Eurocentric "healthy plate." While we may not use beets, we love cooking with lotus root, a root high in fiber, minerals, and vitamins. While we don't traditionally eat Brussels sprouts, one of my mom's favorite vegetables is bitter melon, a nutrient-dense vegetable that has been linked to reducing blood sugar.

Unfortunately, this disconnect between cultural groups and mainstream health narratives is not uncommon. At the *New York Times* event "The Future of Food" on October 30th, activist and farmer Kristyn Leach described her experience investigating health disparities within elderly Asian American populations. One example was of a Chinese grandmother who refused to eat broccoli, despite being told by dieticians that she needed to eat more vegetables. However, after conversing with her in her native language and asking her the right questions, the dieticians realized that while she didn't want broccoli, she did want gai lan, a Chinese cultivar of broccoli.

"Actually listening to people makes a difference in health outcomes," Leach said. "Instead of talking down to people, listen to what they really know. We can improve the stark health disparities that people face by starting from the ground up."

This person-centric approach is vital when working with different ethnic groups, especially given that chronic conditions such as diabetes and obesity disproportionately affect people of color. Evidence suggests that integrating cultural competency into health education improves diabetes outcomes and patient satisfaction. Wholesome, nutritious foods have real power and potential to change the impact of chronic illnesses, but only if they can fit into the cultural context of the person eating those foods.

Why Is This Disconnect Happening?

When you do an internet search for healthy recipes, what results appear? A lot of kale salads, grilled chicken breast, and quinoa bowls. A typical image of the USDA's MyPlate consists of half a plate of fruits and vegetables, like broccoli and apple slices, a palm-size portion of lean protein like chicken, and a grain like brown rice. In addition, health and wellness companies fixate on the idea that a thin Caucasian woman doing yoga in the park and smiling over a bowl of spinach is the picture of health.

People of color are constantly bombarded with the notion that Eurocentric eating patterns are the only option for a healthy diet. Not only are these unfamiliar foods often unappealing, but they are also isolating. "It almost puts shame on their own cultural foods, because they feel like they have to give up foods they love just so they can be healthy," Nazima Qureshi, a dietician who works with South Asian and Middle Eastern Muslim women, told the *Washington Post*.

Moreover, asking people to switch over to a completely different diet is unsustainable. Food is more than sustenance; what ingredients are used, how the dish is prepared, and how it is consumed are integral parts of cultural identity, heritage, and tradition. Prescribing a diet that doesn't adhere to these customs makes it difficult for people to adopt long-term. In order to drive lasting change in health, it is crucial that nutrition education allows people to practice their food culture and customs.

How Do We Resolve This?

Representation matters. When health marketing only promotes thin, affluent Caucasians and when popular recipes only include ingredients from one part of the world, it excludes people who do not identify with this narrative. Moreover, 78% of dieticians in the US are white, whereas only 60% of US citizens are white. This lack of diversity within the nutrition field makes it all the more important for current dieticians to become familiar with different food cultures.

For example, Wendy Lopez, co-founder of Food Heaven Made Easy, told *Self*, "Oftentimes, I get clients who feel defeated because they don't want to leave behind the tortillas or plantains, but think it's something they have to do in the name of good health. I use this as an opportunity to shift the conversation and provide education on all the amazing foods they can enjoy, that not only benefit their health, but are also culturally relevant." To effectively engage with the patient in a way that is culturally sensitive, it's important to ask the right questions:

- What do they usually eat? People are less likely to eat healthy if it requires them to change their entire grocery list.
- What are their financial limitations? Not every family can afford organic kale and cage-free chicken.
- Where do they buy their food? If they shop at an ethnic grocery store, it's important to be familiar with those common ingredients.
- What is their typical schedule? People with tight school or work schedules will have more difficulty keeping fresh produce or preparing time-consuming meals.
- Who do they live with? The people in the household can change their mealtime patterns and behaviors.
- Where do they live? While going for a walk or run is commonly recommended as exercise, not everyone feels safe on the streets of their neighborhood.
- Do they have religious food practices? For example, those who practice fasting for religious purposes limit their ability to follow certain diet plans.

In addition, using images of ethnic families and speaking a common language are hugely relevant and impactful for people of different cultures. Being able to identify with the health information they receive is significant to feeling comfortable and understood, which in turn supports their ability to make healthier choices on their own terms.

How Does Food Culture Play Into Plant-Based Meats?

At the *New York Times'* event, Rebekah Moses from Impossible Foods—which makes plant-based "meat" products—also offered a unique perspective on the importance of food culture. "Beef is delicious," she said. "It's important for certain food cultures, and telling people to stop eating it seems patriarchal. However, if you provide a consumer alternative using a commodity soy product that is healthy and sustainable and can be true to food culture, that's a net positive." Instead of asking meat-eaters to give up beef and eat salads, Moses is suggesting that a plant-based burger—which looks, feels, and tastes like meat—is a more effective and realistic option for meat-eaters who are looking for healthier diets. And it's working: Moses reports that 95% of their customers also eat meat and dairy, meaning that their product is not one that only attracts vegetarians.

Just as how recommending bok choy to a Chinese family is providing them with a culturally relevant healthy option, Impossible Foods aims to provide healthier, more sustainable meat products to consumers who already eat meat. When we meet people where they're at, rather than try to completely alter their diet, we can find success in creating a healthier society.

4

Addressing Wellness in the Workplace Requires a Dedicated Effort from Employers

Deborah Teplow

Deborah Teplow leads and co-founded the Institute for Wellness Education. She is an expert in the field and has previously served as a director on the board for the Global Alliance for Medical Education.

Prioritizing wellness in the workforce isn't just about providing gym passes and offering healthy snacks. Employers need to recognize that the workplace environment is also crucial to all employees' well-being. Starting to focus on the work culture means asking the right questions. For example, how is the company prioritizing the health of its employees? Is the company really promoting a wellness culture by taking actual steps, small and big? Are each employee's needs being met individually? Those are important questions for employers to consider when prioritizing wellness to curb the driving costs of poor employee health.

Employers are under intense pressure to rein in costs and increase profitability. This is particularly true when it comes to developing employer-sponsored wellness programs.

As a result, employers focus their time and money on identifying and trying to fix the obvious causes of poor employee health (smoking, overeating, lack of exercise, and so forth) that are driving up costs.

"How to Create a Workplace Culture of Wellness," by Dr. Deborah Teplow, Dotdash publishing family. Reprinted by permission.

Unfortunately, in part, this is an example of missing the forest for the trees. Yes, employees need to address these unhealthy lifestyle habits. But, it's how, when, and why employers address them that determine the likelihood of success.

Creating a Wellness Culture Means Doing More

To create a healthy, high-performance workforce, employers will have to dig deeper to identify and address the many and varied factors that affect their employees and influence their health and wellness.

Ultimately, this means that employers will also have to examine the role that workplace culture plays in employees' overall well-being because health and wellness don't happen in a vacuum. We know that social factors play a significant role in peoples' well-being.

For most employers, creating a culture of health and wellness isn't just a matter of choosing the right gym program, introducing a dynamite team challenge, or changing the cafeteria menu. It's a matter of making sure that health and wellness are woven into the cultural fabric of the organization.

It's both about what the organization does and who the organization is—what the organization stands for, what its mission is, and how its approach to caring for its employees is expressed. Making a culture shift to one that supports health and wellness is a significant change, but can deliver measurable benefits quickly.

How to Change the Wellness Culture

The first thing organizations can do to start the culture shift is to make sure that health and wellness are part of their corporate values and that those values are clearly defined and expressed.

This includes both policies and practices and is revealed in everything the organization does, from small to large. Even something as small as whether you have veggie slices or donuts (or in addition to donuts) at your next meeting sets the tone and communicates your intent.

The second thing is to recognize that each organization is a unique ecosystem in which each individual plays a role and exerts influence, whether consciously or unconsciously, overtly or covertly. Therefore, the value of caring about individuals is important.

People need to know that they count and that you care about them as individuals, not simply as programmers, welders, clerks, or teachers.

Creating a Wellness Culture

To optimize the health and wellness of employees, take note of the following three priorities. They will lead you on the path to employee wellness.

Recognize That Health and Wellness Require Effort from Both the Grassroots and the Executive Suite

Health and wellness thrive as a team sport, in which everyone at every level has a role to play. Employees talk about health and wellness as a critical personal and organizational imperative in a wellness supporting culture. People at the top lead and commit to health and wellness, such that wellness activities receive support from the top levels of management, who also model the values.

Create Conditions That Allow Your Employees to Shine

Employers should do whatever it takes to make the environment around the office attractive for wellness. Employers need to make the office a place employees want to work because they end each day with a feeling of accomplishment, a feeling that their efforts count, and that they are valued.

This means fostering employees' sense of autonomy, mastery, control, and meaning. Realizing that your employees are your most important asset can make all the difference. Create a healthy environment and your team can flourish.

Reach People Where They Are

Don't force-feed pre-packaged wellness solutions to employees you care about. Meet your employees where they are currently and demonstrate that you care by helping them take steps to achieve the goals that are important to them.

By helping employees achieve what's important to them, you also help them build competency and orient them for success. You help them prove to themselves that positive change is possible.

Paying for a gym membership or a fitness band is great for people who are already committed to working out, but it will never reach people who are not committed or easily motivated to exercise. Unhealthy behaviors may be coping responses to issues that aren't directly related to what you see as the problem.

The Bottom Line for Employee Wellness Initiatives

To successfully promote workforce wellness and enjoy its benefits, care about employees, and support and help them achieve what counts for them. You then will have a far greater likelihood of getting them onboard for other changes that can help them and your bottom line.

Taking cultural change seriously; making the workplace an environment that supports people's initiative, creativity, responsibility, and meaning; and helping employees address issues with which they struggle are the real building blocks to creating a workplace that reflects great health and wellness that is also self-sustaining.

5

Workplaces Can Be Redesigned to Promote Employee Wellness

Libby Sander

Libby Sander is assistant professor of organizational behavior at Bond Business School, Bond University, in Australia.

While many employers have concluded that it is in their best interest to care about the health of their employees, it might not be enough to offer programs and incentives that may not be taken advantage of. The workplace itself can be altered to maximize the health and wellness of those who use its space. This can include lighting and air quality as well as floor plans that encourage employees to move around. Investing in healthy environments could save companies money in the end, when productivity and insurance costs are factored in.

Companies spend tens of billions of dollars each year on wellness programs—on gyms, health funds, yoga classes, and the like. But research shows only mixed success, with low take-up rates among employees and a poor return on investment for companies.

People attending work while sick costs the Australian economy about A$34.1 billion each year through lost productivity.

"How Employers Can Design Workplaces to Promote Wellness," by Libby Sander, The Conversation, February 21, 2018. https://theconversation.com/how-employers-can-design-workplaces-to-promote-wellness-91983. Licensed under CC BY-4.0.

Rather than promoting these wellness programs, companies should instead design the workplace itself to support wellness. Sleep pods, air filtered by green walls, and selectively placed healthy food are already realities in some workplaces.

Through this kind of design, employees are "opted-in" to an environment that supports their health and well-being during the day. They don't have to choose to take a walk at lunchtime or think about taking the stairs. The design of the workplace is engineered around creating these positive choices.

It isn't just "presenteeism" (showing up to work in spite of medical problems such as back pain, headaches, or mental health issues) that is a problem. The cost of absenteeism in Australia is estimated at A\$7 billion a year.

Meanwhile, the prevalence of chronic disease including obesity, diabetes and heart disease continues to rise among the workforce.

Modern work practices contribute to these diseases through the largely sedentary nature of modern office work. Increased sitting, for example, has been associated with higher risk of chronic disease.

Wellness Programs That Work

Wellness programs have become increasingly popular as companies and researchers have realised that productivity lies in the health of individual workers. The focus has also shifted to prevention of health problems rather than treating them after the fact.

Traditionally, this was accomplished by offering a range of services, from discounted health fund and gym memberships, and medical screening services, to activity-based programs such as in-house massages and yoga classes.

But simply giving employees lots of information about their health and telling them what to do doesn't work. Research has shown that these programs don't often change behaviour or help us to build new habits. If we are faced with too many choices, for example, our self control is quickly depleted.

So instead of simply presenting employees with options that are good for us, companies can borrow from behavioural economics and "nudge" us to change our behaviour.

Many workplaces are already using this design, covering a range of factors including lighting, air quality, materials, furniture, physical activity, and food.

Take the stairs, for example. In traditional offices lifts are generally positioned centrally, making them the easiest option. If you wanted to take the stairs that often means using the fire stairs, with the added risk that you might be locked out when you try to re-enter on another floor.

By simply moving the staircase into a central position you can make them the most convenient option for quickly moving between floors. This is common practice now at a wide variety of companies such as the Boston Consulting Group's New York offices.

But let's not stop there. By using experience design, employees can be incentivised in other ways to take the stairs.

Timber walls, natural lighting, art and music can be used to align with our natural preferences for attractive and calming environments, and nudge employees to take the stairs. At the offices of Delos in New York, sensors in the stairs record the number of trips employees take during the day.

Every time an employee uses the stairs, a drop of water is added to an electronic "waterfall" display. The more times you take the stairs, the bigger the waterfall gets.

This use of technology represents a bit of gamification within the workplace. It's like a scorecard for stair use, and every trip comes with a visual reward that gradually adds up.

By creating well-designed, centrally located eating areas and providing healthy food choices, organisations can also encourage employees to make better food choices.

In one study researchers from Yale teamed up with Google to try and nudge employees towards healthy choices. Simple changes in the office cafe had huge results. Replacing loose M&Ms with small packages reduced serving sizes by 58%, and putting up prominent signs increased the number of employees eating certain vegetable dishes by 74%.

Research also shows that air quality and lighting at work can have significant effects on brain function and productivity. Poor oxygen levels, toxic gases from furniture, and toxic chemicals are commonplace in modern workplaces, while poor lighting can cause headaches, eye strain, and tiredness.

Workplaces can be designed to counter some of these problems, by using circadian lighting systems for instance. Circadian lighting follows the patterns of natural light over the course of a day. Sleepy in the morning? The system will provide the right amount of light to wake you up. Circadian lighting results in your body releasing melatonin at the right times, helping employees unwind after work and improving sleep quality.

Using air filtration systems, as well as materials and furniture that don't contain chemicals like formaldehyde, can significantly contribute to employees' well-being and productivity. Providing natural ventilation, views of nature, and greenery in the workplace have also been shown to improve employee's wellbeing and productivity.

Investing in office design has been seen as a "nice to have," but the research shows it can also be seen as an investment. The costs of employee illness and lost productivity are high and even simple changes can have huge impact.

And while employees may be concerned about companies designing environments to engineer behavioural choices, this inclusion of behavioural insights is widespread, and can be seen in areas as diverse as city planning and retail.

By providing environments that support and encourage employee well-being organisations can ensure that well-being is not something that people have to make a choice to opt-in on.

6

Wellness Can Help Control Health Care Costs

Ui May Tan

Dr. Ui May Tan is the medical director of the Dublin Marathon and a health and well-being clinical lead at Voluntary Health Insurance.

Chronic diseases, a category that now includes cancer, drive up health care costs and exasperate national economies. Therefore, it is very important for organizations and individuals to prioritize wellness. The World Health Organization describes wellness as the process of "becoming aware of and making choices toward a healthy and fulfilling life." There are different kinds of wellness, including physical wellness, nutritional wellness, emotional wellness, and workplace wellness, all of which the author describes below. In workplace environments especially, employers and employees need to give a high priority to wellness as a long-term investment.

An overview of Irish demographics tells us that the average age of Ireland's population will increase significantly over the next 20 years (by as much as 85%). It is projected to be the fastest increase in Europe. Add to this the projected upturn of 40% in the incidence of chronic disease between 2007 and 2020 (cancer is now categorised as a chronic disease). This will result in increasing healthcare costs and significant impacts not just on the healthcare systems but also for our health in general.

"Why Is Wellness So Important?" by Ui May Tan, Office Worker Health, July 11, 2018. Reprinted by permission.

Before we venture in to why wellness is so important, we should at least reflect on the meaning of wellness. As you can imagine, it isn't an easy concept to define. The word is used in our everyday language with the assumption that everyone knows what it means. The WHO (World Health Organisation) defines wellness as: "an active process of becoming aware of and making choices toward a healthy and fulfilling life. Wellness is more than being free from illness, it is a dynamic process of change and growth…a state of complete physical, mental, and social well-being, and not merely the absence of disease or infirmity."

The concept of wellness isn't just hard to define, there are also many pillars associated with it which makes it difficult when it comes to initiating a programme to promote it. If you search for wellness on the internet, results will show you certain institutions highlight that wellness encompasses at least four pillars and some even extend this to eight pillars. When you dive deeper into the subject you will find an overlap between physical, nutritional, emotional, environmental, social, spiritual and financial pillars. I am not going to touch on every area of wellness but will explain the pillars which will impact us the most.

Physical Wellness

When we talk about physical wellness, I'm quite sure the first thing that pops into your mind is exercise. Regular physical activity is a very important area that we cannot ignore, however our body needs more than movement alone. Sleep, hygiene and of course nutrition are all part of physical wellness.

Nutritional Wellness

While nutrition is tied to physical wellness, it is such an important area that it is also a pillar in its own right. Nutritional requirements are based on age, gender, activity level and body chemistry; strengthening this pillar requires careful attention to one's diet. Based on research we know that nutritional improvements will help strengthen the other pillars of holistic health and wellness.

Emotional Wellness

The final wellness pillar that impacts us the most is emotional wellness. This encompasses the ability to navigate feelings, by identifying, assessing and effectively sharing those feelings with others. We all have ups and downs in life which most of the time whisk us through an emotional journey. The better you understand and manage your feelings, the smoother the journey will be. By opening up and navigating your feelings, you actually improve your social wellness. Sharing true feelings helps us connect with others and form positive relationships.

Social relationships create support systems that can carry us through life's struggles. Harvard's Study of Adult Development ran for 80 years, collecting data on hundreds of participants. A recent study on a subset of this population—surviving octogenarians— investigated the connections between marital satisfaction, social lives, and happiness. Researchers found that participants who spent more time with others reported greater levels of happiness. When the demands of life increase and stress mounts, the ability to turn to someone for support and understanding is powerful.

So now back to the question of "Why Is Wellness So Important?" Understanding the explanations of the pillars of wellness above is one thing; practicing them is a completely different story. Considering how much time we spend at work, it's not surprising that workplace environments and culture can negatively impact our physical and mental well-being, however it's also worth bearing in mind that work is actually good for our health. It provides employees with self-esteem, social inclusion and financial reward.

Research consistently shows that when employees feel their work is meaningful and they are valued and supported, they tend to have higher wellbeing levels, be more committed to an organisation's goals and, crucially, they perform better also. It is therefore imperative that employers implement pro-active measures to promote physical and psychological well-being amongst their employees.

Workplace Wellness

Wellness programmes or initiatives are created or organised to embrace the above pillars and to promote physical and psychological well-being at the workplace. In the past, wellness programmes may have been seen as something that was nice to offer employees. Now many companies understand that health and wellness is a strategic imperative for their business that helps them take a dent out of rising health care costs. These programmes assist employers in resolving health-related productivity and performance issues, and ultimately save the organisation money.

Direct healthcare costs are relatively easy for employers to identify; however, many organisations don't realise the impact that indirect costs have on their workplace. Things such as sick days and the effect of presenteeism—the cost of employees who are on the job, but not fully working due to illness and medical conditions—can be sizeable and harder for small businesses to absorb. In fact, one study of 50,000 workers from 10 different employers showed that lost productivity costs related to absenteeism and presenteeism were 2.3 times higher than medical and pharmacy costs. A Rand study published in 2014, Do Workplace Wellness Programs Save Employers Money, examined 10 years of data from a Fortune 100 employer's wellness programme. When compared against the lifestyle-management component, disease management delivered 86% of the hard health care cost savings, generating US$136 in savings per member, per month and a 30% reduction in hospital admissions.

At-risk employees suffer from factors like obesity, blood pressure, diabetes, and depression, which can lead to costly (and avoidable) health claims. At-risk people should be identified through personal health assessments and biometric testing, and encouraged—not coerced—to participate in personalised care-management programmes to minimise their chances of becoming chronically ill.

Conclusion

So, despite the fact there are many wellness programmes organised in workplaces, engagement rates are often poor. Do employees simply not care about their health and wellbeing? That's unlikely, but perhaps they are hoping for a "quick fix" and don't see the long term benefits of investing in their wellness over time?

To address this, the basic goal of a workplace wellness programme should always be to promote the lifelong benefits of long term thinking and investment in wellness by both employees AND employers.

7

Wellness Is Important to Living a More Fulfilling Life

Judy Molinaro

Judy Molinaro is a corporate wellness consultant and the author of Eat Like You Give a Damn.

Taking care of oneself is crucial. Everyone should take care of not only their health but also their well-being. Health is the process of making sure the body is at its best self, free of disease and injury. Wellness goes a little deeper. It encompasses making changes to one's lifestyle to live a better life. There are many things a person can do to improve both their health and wellness. Actions include nurturing their spirit, quieting their mind, and building their body.

With access and affordability to health insurance hanging in the balance, it's more important than ever to take care of your mind, body and spirit.

With today's technology and superior level of healthcare in the United States you may be asking why you should be so concerned? Why is health and wellness so important?

What Is the Difference Between Health and Wellness?

Health focuses on the physical and mental body being free from illness, injury, or disease. Health is a goal you work to achieve. For example, managing chronic conditions such as lowering

"Why Is Wellness So Important," by Judy Molinaro, Joomla, October 29, 2018. Reprinted by permission.

your blood pressure or controlling diabetes are goals to be reached, as are losing weight or strengthening your heart through cardiovascular exercise.

Many chronic diseases, like hypertension and type 2 diabetes, are on the rise. The most frightening statistic is that they are becoming more commonplace in young children. Often these diseases are a result of unhealthy eating habits and increased weight gain.

Dietary habits established in childhood often carry into adulthood. Today, about one in three American kids and teens are overweight or obese and the prevalence of obesity in children has more than tripled from 1971 to 2011. Teaching children how to eat healthy at a young age will help them stay healthy throughout their life.

Wellness is more than being free from illness, it is the spirited process of change and growth that lasts for a lifetime. Wellness addresses the broader spectrum of your body encompassing the overall balance of your physical, mental, and spiritual well-being. It speaks to the way you live your everyday life. It is not an end to be achieved, rather it is a lifestyle that you adopt.

Maintaining an optimal level of wellness is absolutely crucial to living a higher of quality life. As a parent it is imperative to cultivate a culture of wellness as a family. Wellness matters! Why does it matter? It matters because your well-being not only effects your emotions, it also effects the emotions of your children.

As a parent, it is important that you set a positive example. Your children's attitudes and actions will model your behavior; it's an ongoing circle. The psychological effects to obese children can be devastating; they are more prone to low self-esteem, negative body image, and depression.

What You Can Do to Improve Overall Health and Wellness

Your body is a direct reflection of what's going on in your mind. In order to be successful improving the quality of your life you must change your mindset.

You can't wait until everything is just right because it never will be. There will always be hurdles to leap and challenges to be faced.

Stop wearing your "busy-ness" like a badge of honor. Stop feeling obligated to be reachable 24/7 by people that have a warped sense of urgency. Stop being hijacked by the needs and desires of others.

Knock it off with all the talk of "The Terrible Too's"; too busy, too tired, too hard, too early etc. You have the ability to control your destiny. Your future is wide open and you can create it by what you chose to do.

Quiet Your Mind

- Love yourself—It's about time you recognize and acknowledge how amazing and unique you are. While it's human nature to want the approval and acceptance of others, don't allow their opinions to define and limit you. Appreciate yourself for who you are and what you have to offer the world. Love yourself from the inside out and everything else will fall into place.
- Be true to yourself—Most often people have no idea where you've been, where you're headed, or where you are in your journey. Focus on the things that make you your happiest, healthiest self. Continue to explore your passions, reach for your goals, and achieve your wildest dreams.
- Stop comparing yourself—Positive self-talk is empowering; know that what you focus on will become your reality. Imagine all the things you could bring to fruition if you channeled your time and energy into positive aspirations. If you realized how powerful your thoughts were you would never want to think a negative thought again.

Build Your Body

- Get fit—Getting fit is a slow and steady process, being fit is not a destination, it is a way of life. Adhering to regularly scheduled workouts will take commitment, determination, and discipline; doing what needs to be done, when it needs to be done, when you don't want to do it.
- Eat well—Every living cell in your body is made from what you eat and drink. If you consistently eat and drink junk food, you will have a junk body. Food is not just calories, it is information; it talks to your DNA and tells it what to do. Food can be your medicine or your poison, choose wisely.
- Sleep soundly—It's important to make sure that you get the rest your body needs. When your body is fully rested and you are getting the deep sleep you require, your hormones will work together and support your overall health and wellness goals.

Nurture Your Spirit

- Pay it forward—When you're kind, you demonstrate to others that they mean something to you. Even if the person is a stranger to you, you are recognizing that their life matters. When you give of yourself openly and freely, your physical and mental health improves exponentially. The smallest gesture or kind word can brighten your day and brings you closer to others.
- Maintain a social network—Socializing has been proven to have a positive impact both physically and mentally and can be the key to a lifetime of wellness. If you're looking to live a long and healthy life, start surrounding yourself with good friends. A study from Brigham Young University found that people with social relationships live 50 percent longer than people who are more socially isolated.
- Live a yogic lifestyle—It's easy to get caught up in the whirlwind of daily life and spend much of your day battling

the challenges laid before you. Adopting a yogic lifestyle means committing to living a meaningful life and interacting with the world around you more mindfully. Embrace yoga's spiritual journey and finding harmony on and off the mat.

Maximize Your Level of Health and Wellness

By quieting your mind, building your body, and nurturing your spirit you will be well on your way to achieving your health and wellness goals. Work toward a state of well-being and you will see your lifestyle begin to improve.

Care for your mind, body and spirit and begin to lessen the occurrences of disease and illness. An enhanced quality of physical and mental fitness is the answer to your question "Why is health and wellness so important?"

8

The Wellness Industry Creates a Toxic and Exclusive Culture

Isabel Salken

Isabel Salken is a writer at the Cavalier Daily *and a student at the University of Virginia.*

The wellness industry promotes a toxic culture where college students are plagued with posts on weight loss and dieting on their social media pages. Those posts are filled with claims based on pseudoscience and backed by a weight loss industry that pushes money into those wellness influencers. They perpetuate the idea that everyone should be involved in some form of dieting, whether a paleo, keto, or gluten-free diet. Moreover, this culture promotes thinness as healthy and normal. It belittles any body shape that doesn't fit this exclusive image of thinness.

The wellness industry has been a smashing success the past few years with a $4.2 trillion market in 2017. Wellness is defined as "the state of being in good health," but has been marred by the industry's commercialization of avocado toast, the elimination of dairy and gluten, intermittent fasting, replacing every grain with cauliflower, using expensive skin care products—the list goes on.

To get a better sense of how the industry impacts college students, I spoke to university students to get an idea of what wellness means to them. Third-year college student Jeanne

"What If the Wellness Industry Is Actually … Bad?" by Isabel Salken, *Cavalier Daily*, December 4, 2019. Reprinted by permission.

Rockwell said she often views "wellness" as how it's defined on her social media.

"Sometimes my popular page can be littered with dieting tactics and weight loss tricks," Rockwell said. "It must sense my self-esteem issues."

Wellness influencers have taken over the space of Instagram in many ways, acquiring sponsors and polluting feeds with posts promoting fad diets, photoshopped bodies, skin care routines and workout regimens, most of the time with no credentials backing their "expertise," they are chosen for being "on brand."

"No-guilt recipes" circulate endlessly on social media, implying that the normal version of said recipe should make you feel guilty. Paleo, keto and gluten-free diets plague social media feeds of those who don't need to be restricting themselves in this way. These diets have gone beyond the necessary dietary restrictions they are for some to become fashionable, trendy fads.

In fact, using diet hashtags has become a commodity in the wellness space on social media because these buzzwords get so much traction. Most influencers in the wellness community are making large amounts of money by posting pictures of herbal teas or health packages. Even micro-influencers—those with 10,000-50,000 followers—can make over $100,000 each year from sponsored posts.

A majority of the claims made by influencers are backed by pseudoscience and diet culture. The wellness industry itself is backed largely by the diet and weight loss industry. These industries are hyperfocused on somehow changing a person or at least a part of them, which only fuels insecurity, and it has worked. Instagram had to ban diet advertisements for fueling negative body image perceptions.

The center of wellness in this regard is weight loss. It indirectly demonizes larger people, practices and food, indoctrinating the idea that "thin" is what it means to be "healthy." In reality, what results from framing unrealistic body standards and overly-promoting clean eating are eating disorders, fatphobia and body shaming—all of which are correlated with depression, body dysmorphia, lower self-esteem and more.

The wellness industry within the media also requires money and is, therefore, highly exclusive. Third-year college student Emily Elmore reflected on the inherently privileged commodities of the wellness community. Not everyone can afford weekly spin classes and $9 green juices.

"Money and time are definitely factors that affect people's motivation to pursue a healthier lifestyle, especially college students," Elmore said.

However, if you're anything like me, you've participated—and continue to participate—in wellness culture. You've been influenced and have, as a result, bought products, adopted new habits and maybe even changed your diet.

But it's not all bad. The industry genuinely helped me find balance in my life in the realm of food and fitness—something I believe everyone should find for themselves. Ironically, both food and fitness practices are central to my life. Eating a diet filled with whole foods works wonders for my body.

It also introduced me to more sustainable, environmentally-friendly practices, which are invaluable during the climate crisis we are facing today. Buying local, organic and even eating meatless when I can has allowed me to support small businesses, divert income from corrupt industries and promote good environmental practices that can help combat climate change. However, there is a difference between engaging in these practices to be sustainable or because you think it's trendy.

Wellness can be promoted without demonizing body types. Instead of focusing on changing your body, you can focus on changing your mind with positive behaviors like getting enough sleep, which has been linked to good health. Sometimes it's OK to just watch Netflix and eat a cookie.

For the longest time, the concept of maintaining proper wellness as perpetuated by the media controlled my life and made me think that doing anything other than what I saw promoted was bad—and that is the problem. It was only by taking a step back and removing myself from the narratives framed by the media that I could begin to acquire agency over my own definition of wellness.

The next time you view "advice" or see products on media connected to wellness, take a step back and think about the motives behind the content you are seeing and the credentials behind those making the assertions. Do your own research—recognize that you are your biggest advocate and can only decide what works best for your body and mind.

Wellness isn't about changing yourself or fitting into a certain idea. Wellness is mental and physical health, recognizing that you don't have to sacrifice one for the other. Wellness should be genderless, classless and raceless. Because above all, wellness is whatever works best for you.

9

Our Obsession with Wellness Is Undermining Feminism

Jen Pavich

Jen Pavich is a feminist life coach who helps women thrive in a male-oriented society.

Wellness culture is troubling, as it associates the pursuit of health with morality. The culture of wellness is deeply rooted in society's capitalist ways. Similar to how poverty applies to one's failure to do better, poor health applies to one's failure to prioritize self-care. In doing so, society relieves itself of all responsibility and blame to do something about national health issues like obesity. Nevertheless, what this mentality refuses to take into consideration is that health is an economic issue. We live in a society where many live under the poverty line and where basic necessities like food are not accessible to all.

Wellness has become a key measure of personal success—just ask the Instagirls. We all know that the image of a successful woman isn't complete without the obligatory performative displays of yoga in exotic locations, expensive organic lunches, or "fresh from the gym" selfies (in full makeup). These images are more than a plea for validation. Not only do they encapsulate a signaling of wealth (and arguably whiteness) that's downright disturbing, but they continue to reinforce the notion that health is something we do, rather than something we may have limited control over.

"Our Obsession with Wellness Is Undermining Feminism (and Costing Us Healthcare)," by Jen Pavich, Medium, January 30, 2019. Reprinted by permission.

The fact is, we've long equated the pursuit of health, particularly as it applies to weight, with morality. As a culture we judge individuals for how much time, energy and money that they devote to maintaining their personal health, often regardless of other factors that might affect an individual's ability to self-care. This attitude is an extension of the myth of individualism that is inextricably woven into our capitalist culture.

Who here has never given a side-eye to an obese person on an airplane or someone lighting a cigarette on a sidewalk? It's easy to be reductive when it comes to personal responsibility and health—especially when we're looking at someone else. Making health into a virtue and disease into something that's brought on by irresponsibility means that we don't have to do anything about it as a society—least of all provide healthcare for our citizens.

The fact is that, as a culture, we're addicted to perfectionism fueled by rugged individualism. We're endlessly infatuated with the notion that everything in our lives, including our health, is a question of personal responsibility. Never mind that our air quality is still killing people and that our water has been poisoned by corporations and negligent government officials that are rarely held accountable. Likewise, the fact that 2.3 million Americans live in a food desert and over 7 million people are working at least two jobs to make ends meet. Health as morality thinking is uncomfortably ableist and health is largely an economic issue. The minor detail that the CDC reports that day-to-day health behaviors, such as diet and exercise, account for less than 25% of differences in health outcomes is not even a blip on our radar. The message is still: we just need to buck up and do more so we can bootstrap our way to better health.

This isn't to say that pursuing personal health goals is necessarily a bad thing but chasing health at all costs (the way our culture programs us to do) is not without consequences. Not only does the pursuit of perfection through "health" lead to discrimination and leaving behind the most vulnerable in our society, there's also a pronounced cost to those who have the resources and ability to chase the dream of perfect health as well.

Eating disorders like orthorexia are on the rise, especially among women. This is hardly a surprise in a culture that tells women that the way they look is the most important thing about them and then links that to an increasingly steep climb to consume only the purest of nutrition.

The multi-billion-dollar beauty and diet industry has spent decades trying to legitimize itself in the face of feminism. The easiest way to do this has been to conflate the concept of physical beauty with the idea of what constitutes health, until the two become so hopelessly entangled that we can't tell the difference. The result is that we (sadly, including many members of the medical community) feel it's a moral imperative to maintain the cultural beauty and weight standard.

The ways this benefits patriarchy and capitalism go far beyond the money we spend. After all, how better to get womxn, even many who identify as feminists, out of the way than to convince them to invest untold amounts of time and money into being half-starved and on a never-ending hamster wheel of pursuing the unachievable? It certainly doesn't leave much left over for smashing the patriarchy so chalk one up for the existing power structure.

It's not that we don't see what's happening. Ask any good feminist and she'll explain to you how fatphobia is real and wrong. She might even point out the token fat celebrity or even a fat activist that she thinks is great. But try asking her (especially if she possesses a "culturally acceptable" body type) how she'd feel about gaining 20 lbs and she'll likely start squirming and equivocating. Feminine conditioning is insidious. We may be able see the problem from an abstract lens and even discount or make fun of it, but that doesn't mean that we're not still internalizing those pictures of salad-eating ecstasy on some level.

Health is determined by a multitude of factors, some of which we may have some influence over, but many of which we don't.

The fact remains, you can't tell how healthy a person is by looking at them. Having a health issue is not a moral failing because personal health is not a moral issue at all. It's just another way to pit the people with the least power against one another in a capitalist patriarchy.

10

The Wellness Industry Promotes Eating Disorders

Jennifer Liles

Jennifer Liles, MSW, LCSW, provides mental health life tips from a social justice perspective. She has a private mental health practice in Independence, Missouri.

Is the wellness industry really trying to make people healthier? The emphasis on ideal bodies and perfect lifestyles may have a detrimental effect on women's health in particular. Shifting the focus away from strict beauty and weight standards toward a culture of love and appreciation for what our bodies can do could be healthier than anything the wellness industry is peddling.

I woke up this morning to this headline from the *New York Times*: "Smash the Wellness Industry: Why are so many smart women falling for its harmful, pseudoscientific claims?" which discusses the author's own struggle with eating disorders. Because the *Times* is behind a paywall, I'll summarize. The author, a novelist named Jessica Knoll spent most of her adult life going on one diet after another, following the advice of dieticians, doctors, and whatever fad of the week diet was being promoted. It wasn't until she found a dietician who supported intuitive eating that her relationship with food started to change. I'll quote Ms. Knoll here:

The new dietitian had a different take. "What a gift," she said, appreciatively, "to love food. It's one of the greatest pleasures in life. Can you think of your appetite as a gift?" It took me a moment to wrap my head around such a radical suggestion. Then I began to cry.

She goes on in the article to quote health resources that link chronic dieting to heart disease and other physical ailments, all of which is important. But for just a moment here, I want to focus on the huge emotion she showed when a professional looked at her and said "your appetite is a gift." That's why I highlighted it.

How I Learned to Treat Eating Disorders

In 2010, I took my first job as a full-time therapist, after decades as a case manager and then a case manager supervisor who did therapy as part of her job duties. It was in a public health setting. On more than one occasion, I went to my supervisor and said "I'm not familiar with this mental health disorder (or this treatment population) at all! What do I do?" See, in public mental health, we often don't have the luxury of referring out to a more experienced person who knows the disorder better, because either that specialist doesn't accept Medicaid, or because they are in a part of the city that costs too much gas to get to, or is too far off the bus lines.

I did this when I was assigned a therapy participant who was severely and actively anorexic and another who had a two-decade pattern of refusing to eat any solids at all. My supervisor reminded me of the facts of life in public mental health, and I ordered a few textbooks on eating disorders treatment (and people wonder why I'm always broke). I then spent a couple of months becoming an expert. Actually, I became an expert almost by accident. Because even those books held to the lie that "thin equals healthy" far too often. (It's beyond the scope of this article, but there is ample scientific evidence that being too thin is more likely to contribute to death than being even "morbidly" obese.)

So I Began to Wing It, and a Funny Thing Happened

I mean, really winging it. Started with some on the spot analysis of what was going on, referred back to the one text that did help, one that provided some guidance for using cognitive behavioral therapy methods in eating disorders therapy, and dove in. I began with the premise that the people I was treating were fundamentally fine just the way they are. And that they need to change their relationships with food before it kills them. So, I talked to them about loving their body and staying away from scales. And listening to their bodies.

I gave them permission to love their bodies, and to love food. Their lives began to change. Some of them had their weights move closer to "normal," and others didn't. But the binge/diet cycle for most of them began to slow down, and more importantly, they began to address the underlying traumas and self-esteem issues and de-focus food from the center of their lives. Their overall physical and mental health began to improve.

I Started Getting New Client Referrals from Dieticians and Eating Disorders Units

Somehow, in my winging it, I had become an actual expert in eating disorders. I was effective. People's lives got better. And I learned something important: We are training people, especially women, to hate their bodies, and it is being done systemically. I remember reading somewhere about a very tiny elderly woman in a nursing home who apologized profusely every time a staff member lifted her into a bath because she was so heavy. Per the story, she was less than a hundred pounds.

And this story wasn't in any way unique. Over and over, people would come to me, mostly women, and talk to me about how "bad" they were for enjoying food. And I had an epiphany: The diet industry, the wellness industry, and the fashion industry don't see women as people. They see women as objects of attraction for heterosexual men first, and only secondarily, if at all, as people with a right to live a full, self-actualized life. In other words, the diet, wellness, and fashion industries are institutionalized misogyny.

Shortly after I had this epiphany, I went to my personal doctor. My labs were perfect. I walked regularly during my lunch hour, ate a lot of good healthy foods, and maybe a few too many sweets. I was and am generally healthy. My BMI was a point or two over the "moderately obese" line. And I mean just barely. And my good cholesterols were slightly elevated. As always, my blood pressure was low normal.

And he started in on how important it was for me to lose weight. I cut him off in mid-sentence. I told him to stop giving me so much business. He looked at me like I was crazy. Then I explained how his focus on weight loss was creating a sea of women who felt gross in their perfectly healthy bodies, who spent days and nights obsessing about weight instead of going about their lives. I told him to knock it off. All the animation went out of his face, and he walked out of the room, clearly stunned.

I don't know if I got through to him. I certainly hope I did. But I have the same message for you that I had for him. Start loving your body, no matter how big or small it is. Start treating it as kindly as you would treat a dear friend. Give it what it needs, and give it treats occasionally and moderately. Listen to it. Buy clothes that fit, instead of clothes you wish would fit. And then go live your lives.

11

Wellness Culture Is Accessible Only to the Wealthy

Daniela Blei

Daniela Blei is a writer and historian based in California. She has written for Smithsonian, *the* Atlantic, *and the* Los Angeles Review of Books.

Wellness culture promises a fulfilled lifestyle, but it is also a deeply exclusive industry. The wellness movement is not a new phenomenon. Even as early as 1891, people were writing about relying on natural remedies like fresh air to cure illnesses and for the pursuit of a holistic lifestyle. But today's wellness culture promotes products and experiences that are unsustainable to most. Moreover, as wellness culture has come to equate health with beauty and an exclusive body image, it has further exasperated society.

On a 1979 edition of *60 Minutes*, Dan Rather declared: "Wellness. There's a word you don't hear every day. It means exactly what you might think it means: the opposite of illness…. It's a movement that is catching on all over the country." Later in the segment, Rather spoke to Dr. John W. Travis, founder of the Wellness Resource Center in Marin County, north of San Francisco. "Just because you aren't sick," Travis told Rather, "you don't have any symptoms, and you could go get a checkup and get a clean bill of health, that doesn't mean that you're well."

"The False Promises of Wellness Culture," by Daniela Blei, ITHAKA, January 4, 2017. Reprinted by permission.

Once associated with the utopian New Age subcultures of places like Marin County and Santa Fe, wellness has gone mainstream. The landscape is crowded with the business of it: juice bars, meditation retreats, detox diets, mindfulness apps, and retailers of downward-dog-friendly Lycra. Gwyneth Paltrow's lifestyle blog Goop, the movement's standard-bearer, was joined last month by Arianna Huffington's Thrive Global, a new wellness platform "addressing a deep need of our modern societies." At schools, hospitals, and even prisons, proponents cite the self-empowering potential of wellness policies, pointing to soaring morale and stress reduction. Wellness programs now span companies and industries across America, promoting health and "self-management strategies" while promising to boost productivity and curb health care costs. There are now wellness consultants, for those who can pay for the privilege of self-improvement, wellness vacations aboard holistic cruises, and even purveyors of wellness for cats and dogs.

The term *wellness* was popularized in the late 1950s by Dr. Halbert L. Dunn, the so-called father of the movement. Writing in the *Canadian Journal of Public Health* in 1959, Dunn defined "high-level wellness," the organizing principle behind his work, as "a condition of change in which the individual moves forward, climbing toward a higher potential of functioning." Dunn drew a distinction between good health—the absence of illness, or the passive state of homeostasis—and wellness as an active, ongoing pursuit. While good health is objective, dictated by the cold, hard truths of modern medicine, Dunn's wellness is subjective, based on perception and "the uniqueness of the individual." Dunn's ideas have gained a steady following, approaching near-ubiquity in the 21st century—in 2015, the global wellness industry was valued at $3.7 trillion.

But without the emergence of Europe's middle classes, without the wealth and leisure afforded by the Industrial Revolution, today's wellness culture wouldn't exist.

In 1891, Louis Kuhne, a resident of Leipzig, Germany, published *The New Science of Healing*, in which he recounted his struggles with pain and chronic illness and how he overcame them. "At first I sought the aid of 'regular practitioners,'" wrote Kuhne, "but without regular result. Neither did I, in truth, feel much confidence in them." Spurning the medical establishment, Kuhne's guide prescribed natural cures for every ailment: fresh air, strict vegetarianism, abstaining from salt and sugar, and taking up hydrotherapy, a combination of steam baths and cold water plunges to rid the body of disease. Kuhne opened a clinic in Leipzig, where he enjoyed a successful career as a health entrepreneur.

The German author was a journeyman-carpenter who lacked medical training, but his book was a best seller, translated into several European languages. Kuhne was hardly a special case; he reflected the zeitgeist. In the late-nineteenth century, many Europeans saw urban, industrial society as degenerative, damaging to body and soul. The modern masses seemed dangerously disconnected from nature. Sedentary white-collar work was unhealthy; the march of technology dehumanizing. Modern medicine wasn't helping either; doctors, now members of a professional practice, treated patients schematically, not as individuals with holistic needs. After 1874, when Germany passed a law mandating smallpox vaccinations, the effects of which historian Claudia Huerkamp examined in the *Journal of Contemporary History*, anti-vaccination activists condemned "poisoning" by the establishment and rallied around alternative medicine, available on an expanding health market.

In the late-nineteenth century, newly prosperous Europeans created a wellness culture that went by another name: "life reform." It consisted of a growing network of groups and organizations whose members, including Louis Kuhne, experimented with vegetarianism, raw food diets, open-air exercise, nudism, spas, and sunbathing. These men and women subscribed to magazines called *Vegetarian Lookout* and *The Natural Doctor*, disavowed white bread and other processed foods, and vacationed at health resorts promising weight loss or a respite from the dizzying pace of modern life. What began as an effort to mitigate the side effects of affluence, namely inactivity and indulgence, transformed the very meaning of health, from not being sick into "a rational, hygienic lifestyle that stressed self-restraint and moderation in all aspects of life," writes Michael Hau, a historian of Germany's life reform movement.

The aesthetic ideal of the lean, muscular body may derive from Greek antiquity, but it was life reformers who turned the well-cared-for physique into a virtue, Hau explains. Good health became synonymous with beauty and self-fulfillment. As Europeans grew more body-conscious, anxieties about physical appearance fueled an insatiable public appetite for self-improvement books. A wellness industry was born, the trappings of which included healthy foods and drinks, the right attire, and retreats to the sanatorium, the exclusive health spa that was dissected in the pages of Thomas Mann's *The Magic Mountain*.

"One of the ironies of the health-consciousness of the period," Hau notes, "was that it perpetuated the feelings of personal inadequacy that gave rise to it." As a new ideal of health filtered into the mainstream, more work was required to achieve it.

But for many life reformers, asceticism was a source of pleasure. Shedding stuffy Victorian garments and taking to the outdoors, they claimed self-liberation and acted on utopian impulses. "Life reform gave its supporters a sense of agency in their own future," explains Hau, amid sweeping economic and social change. The body became a source of autonomy and self-determination, at least for those men and women who had the resources to cultivate it. Friedrich Bilz, a German author, naturopath, and founder of a health spa near Dresden, sold 3.5 million copies of his health advice book, which was translated into 12 languages. It touted the joys of healthy eating and exercise as well as the freeing possibilities of going barefoot. His book featured letters—stories of personal transformation—that confirmed the bourgeois work ethic: In the modern world, relentless striving was the recipe for success.

Doctors also participated in nineteenth-century wellness culture. Ferdinand Hueppe, a physician who, in the 1880s, worked in the laboratory of Robert Koch (the founder of modern bacteriology), left basic science to study exercise and to promote the benefits of physical activity in schools and white-collar workplaces, both of which required long periods of being seated. In 1899, Hueppe published the *Manual of Hygiene*, one of the first works of exercise physiology, a field that was coming into its own by 1904, when Danish gymnastics educator J.P. Müller pioneered My System, a 15-minute daily workout that could be performed almost anywhere (with visible results!). A hit across Europe, it became the favored fitness regimen of a young, health-conscious Franz Kafka.

Doctors were also health entrepreneurs, establishing sanatoria, yesterday's version of today's Canyon Ranch, where, for a hefty daily fee, patients focused on recovering from illness and overcoming their alienation from nature. Lodgings were often luxurious, but open-air exercise and even manual labor were prescribed, explains Hau. At places like Dr. Ehrenwall's Sanatorium in Germany's Rhineland, patients carved wood and worked with leather outdoors. Writing in 1924 in *The American Journal of Nursing*, Mary Campbell, an American nurse, observed that in recent years, health had become a commodity. "In the present instance the product is health," she explained. "The set-up for business is: the sanatorium, the wholesale house; the patients, the retailers." Through consumption, nineteenth-century wellness culture promised health and, by extension, success and personal fulfillment.

Do economic pressures explain the reemergence of wellness culture? The beginning of the twenty-first century shares some of the defining features of the end of the nineteenth: a technology revolution, capitalist expansion, wealth concentration, labor insecurity, and with it, status anxiety. As early as 1959, Dunn echoed nineteenth-century fears of modernity's ill effects. "As people are crowded closer and closer together in urban living, freedom of action becomes progressively restricted," he noted, pointing to "rampant population increase" and "higher mobility" as barriers to high-level wellness. But Dunn's ideas started off with a small audience; it took decades before Oprah, Dr. Oz, and other popularizers of wellness were propelled to celebrity.

More recently, feminist scholars have examined constructions of health by looking at popular culture, drawing similar conclusions to those of historians of nineteenth-century wellness. Bodily self-improvement is often "conflated with questions of aesthetics, sexuality, and consumerism," according to Carol-Ann Farkas, whose research surveys wellness magazines such as *Self* and *Men's Health*. Writing in *Studies in Popular Culture*, Farkas revisits feminist criticisms of wellness culture as "a radical turning inward of agency toward the goal of transformation of one's own body, in contrast to a turning outward to mobilize for collective action." For Farkas, the key moment was not Dunn's 1959 formulation of high-level wellness, but Oprah's "put on your oxygen mask first," her entreaty to prioritize the self before tending to others.

Feminist critics of wellness culture make a strong case for what's wrong with it, but the embodiment of social problems isn't new. In 1905, Europeans talked about neurasthenia instead of "clean eating," and sipped Sinalco, a healthy alternative to alcohol, instead of cold-pressed juices. Life reform refined bourgeoisie sensibilities and was often expensive, like purchasing a Vitamix or enrolling in the latest boutique fitness class. Far more consequential was that life reformers, in pursuit of a more natural, disciplined lifestyle, blended health with beauty. It didn't take long before a person's outward appearance was taken as an indication of their physical, spiritual, and mental health, a development that would have dangerous, even deadly, consequences. Wellness culture has promised success for more than a century, success in the struggle for survival through bodily control and self-discipline. The modern world is a Darwinian place: As long as there is disenchantment with it, there will be the false redemption of wellness.

12

Obesity Is Costly to the US Economy

J. Michael Gonzalez-Campoy

J. Michael Gonzalez-Campoy is the medical director and chief executive officer of the Minnesota Center for Obesity, Metabolism, and Endocrinology.

The Centers for Disease Control describes obesity as an epidemic. Thirty-five percent of Americans are considered obese. California, Colorado, and Hawaii are the states with the lowest percentages of obesity. However, they all carry a rate above 20 percent. Mississippi and West Virginia have the highest rate at 35 percent. The disease is so prevalent that it puts a strain on health care costs, income, and the workforce. Estimated health care costs relating to obesity in America are in the hundreds of billions of dollars.

Obesity has become a serious health problem in the United States (US): nearly 35% of Americans have obesity. Obesity is not just a problem of "girth control"; it is now considered a chronic disease by the American Medical Association, the American Association of Clinical Endocrinologists, the American College of Endocrinology, the Endocrine Society, the Obesity Society, the American Society of Bariatric Physicians, and the National Institutes of Health (NIH).

It is, in fact, a national epidemic according to the Centers for Disease Control and Prevention (CDC). And it is not just a

"Obesity in America: A Growing Concern," by J. Michael Gonzalez-Campoy, EndocrineWeb, Remedy Health Media, LLC. Reprinted by permission.

weight problem: it can have serious effects on a person's physical, metabolic and psychological health.

Overweight and Obesity Defined

Overweight and obesity are defined by the body mass index (BMI), which is calculated by dividing the weight (in kilograms) by the square of the height (in meters). A BMI of 25 to 29.9 kg/m^2 indicates that an individual has overweight; a BMI of 30 kg/m^2 or more indicates that a person has obesity. People with a BMI greater than 40 kg/m^2 are considered to have stage 3 obesity, and at one time were said to have "morbid obesity." However, BMI is not a perfect measurement; it does not distinguish lean mass from fat mass, nor does it take into account racial or ethnic differences.

Other factors to be considered include waist and neck circumference, overall fitness, and lifestyle. And importantly, the concept that patients may develop "sick fat," or adipose tissue disease (adiposopathy), as introduced into the medical literature by Dr. Harold Bays, now makes it a treatment goal to return adipose tissue function to normal.

In children, obesity is assessed differently. Since a child's body composition varies as he or she ages, it is measured as an age- and sex-specific percentile for BMI. In children and adolescents aged 2 to 19 years, a BMI at or above the 85th, but lower than the 95th, percentile indicates overweight; a child with a BMI at or above the 95th percentile is considered to have obesity.

How Prevalent Is the Problem?

Obesity is widespread, according to the CDC. Using data from the 2011–2012 National Health and Nutrition Examination Survey (NHANES) database, the CDC reported that more than one-third (34.9% or 78.6 million) of US adults have obesity.

As of 2013, according to the CDC, not one state had an obesity prevalence of less than 20%—and the national goal is 15%. The lowest rates (20–25%) were in California, Colorado, Hawaii, Massachusetts, Montana, Utah, Vermont, and Washington, DC.

The highest (35% or higher) were in Mississippi and West Virginia. Regionally, the South had the highest prevalence (30.2%), while the West had the lowest (24.9%).

One independent study of metropolitan areas in the United States revealed that the Provo-Orem, UT area had the lowest incidence of obesity (on a score of 1 to 100, with 1 being the lowest) and the Shreveport-Bossier City, LA area had the highest. The New York metropolitan area is in the middle, with a score of 54.

At the greatest risk for obesity are Hispanics and non-Hispanic black women (30.7% and 41.9%, respectively). Obesity is more prevalent in middle-aged adults, aged 40 to 59 years (39.5%) than in those aged 20 to 39 years (30.3%), or those aged 60 years or older (35.4%). Women with higher incomes are less likely to have obesity than those with lower incomes. Although no correlation has been found between obesity and education in men, women with college degrees are less likely to have obesity than those with less education.

What Is the Impact of Obesity on Society?

Obesity has taken a toll on health care costs across the country—estimated between $147 billion and $210 billion in direct and indirect health care costs, as of 2010.

- Medical costs for individuals with obesity were calculated to be $1429 higher in 2006 than for those of normal weight.
- Lifetime medical costs for a 10-year-old child with obesity are staggering: about $19,000 compared with a child of normal weight.
- When multiplied by the number of 10-year-olds with obesity in America, lifetime health care expenses are estimated to be $14 billion.

In the Workplace

In the workplace, decreased productivity and increased absenteeism due to overweight and obesity is a huge economic burden on our society. Absenteeism related to obesity costs an estimated $4.3 billion per year, and lower productivity on the job costs $506 per employee with obesity each year. The greater an individual's BMI, the higher the number of sick days and medical claims—and a worker's medical costs also increase with obesity. In addition, employees with obesity have higher workers' compensation claims.

Costs More than Financial

If the incidence of obesity continues to climb, combined health care costs associated with treating obesity-related diseases could rise by $48 billion to $66 billion per year by 2030; the loss in productivity could total between $390 billion and $580 billion per year.

The cost is more than just financial, however. Obesity can lead to early mortality and increased susceptibility to other diseases, and can have an incalculable impact on quality of life, as well as on the family.

13

Fatphobia Is a Big Issue in Our Society

Mary Ali

Mary Ali is a writer based in Australia.

The body positive movement, pioneered by Lizzo, Rihanna, Tess Holliday, and Ashley Graham, among others, receives a lot of backlash in the media. Lizzo, for one, receives a lot of negative messages online because she does not fit the body image that people believe should be the norm. Fatphobia is a real issue. Because thinness is associated with morality, those who do not fit the criteria are automatically deemed immoral. Moreover, fatphobia mostly affects women. It is always women who get trolled for their body. No one trolls Jack Black for being "obese."

Body positivity has been a trending movement for a decade or so now. It has centred on the idea of all individuals loving and accepting their body, regardless of whether they meet societal standards of beauty. Its pioneers include Lizzo, Rihanna, Ashley Graham and Tess Holliday. However, there has been a backlash in the media about these women, particularly Lizzo, for supposedly promoting "unhealthy body standards" that apparently influence people to "become fat" and "develop diabetes."

Now, horrible people say horrible things about celebrities all the time, so it's not often that I pay attention to what people write online. Flicking through Instagram, I liked Taylor Swift's post about her cats, rolled my eyes at an obligatory follow, and

"Lizzo and the Politics of Body Positivity Movements," by Mary Ali, Fashion Industry Broadcast, March 7, 2020. https://fashionindustrybroadcast.com/2020/03/07/lizzo-and -the-politics-of-body-positivity-movements/. Licensed under CC BY-ND.

watched my close friends' Insta-stories. One of Lizzo's multiple posts also displayed itself on my feed. I didn't think much of it. A powerful, unapologetic woman asking her followers to recite "Today's meditation: anything that I've done I cannot un-do. I forgive myself and move forward. There is life after love and love after life." I've never been good at wholeheartedly accepting self-love mantras and wholesome appreciation posts, so it was kind of jarring to see on my phone. The thing that really stopped me though? The comments on her post.

In their unedited, original form (yes, I know there are typos and grammatic errors—it's taken everything in me not to fix them) here are some awful ones:

> "yeah cause promoting obesity is mentally and physically healthy #diabetes."

> "breaking news: 7 earthquakes happen in every continent. Australia has been destroyed. possible armageddon. source of these disasters from the usa. terrorist attack from lizzo suspected."

> "Didn't know they sold whale sized clothing."

> "We are not interested in seeing your body. Dont even try to promote this useless type of body shape cos you will fail and u have failed. This type of body and look is nothing good. I dont wish my faughter and female member of my family become shapeless like this and look unhealthy."

> "if diabetes wore a bathing suit."

> This particularly visceral one: "you probably have dead animals in those rolls."

I was shocked when I read them. I thought to myself, "god, people really do suck." Never, in my wildest dreams did I expect to hear people in my life say really similar things. The guy I very briefly went out with earlier this year offhandedly made comments about Lizzo's performance at Sydney's FOMO Festival. He mentioned that "she got plenty of fat" and "she a big bitch." It's safe to say the date that followed was the last.

After sending an article about Lizzo's volunteer work at FoodBank in Australia to my family's chat, a fight with my brother ensued. I should put some kind of disclaimer here: my brother is a sweet person who I would defend with my life, so I was gobsmacked by one of his remarks. He declared "she's overrated, has no talent, and appeals to depressed girls who have serious self esteem issues and need a fat woman to make them feel better." I have never heard such awful things come out of my brother's mouth. Of course, I set him straight and he has since apologised for his heat-of-the-moment remark. Apologising doesn't take back what he said, but it's a start.

This was when I realised that these weren't isolated opinions belonging only to the hateful general public. People in my life also held these beliefs. The thing is, I can't work out why. Is it because these unapologetic women dare to be something other than the accepted norm? That there is a kind of moral value to being thin? That people hate what they can't control? Lizzo recently declared "I know that I'm shocking, because you've never seen, in a long time, a body like mine doing whatever it wants to do and dressing the way that it dresses and moving the way that it moves."

I think one of the major problems is that of "fatphobia" where moral value is attributed to being "thin" and the misconception that weight is an indication of health. Here's the thing, we have detrimentally come to accept the ideology that how you look is a clear signifier of health, but fat doesn't equal unhealthy. Let's think about it, if Lizzo was truly unhealthy, and "on the verge of a heart attack," could she sing, dance and perform for over an hour and a half on stage? Probably not.

Meanwhile, Taylor Swift confessed that when she was at her thinnest: "I thought that I was just like supposed to feel like I was going to pass out at the end of a show, or in the middle of it…I thought that was how it was." I'm a size six (occasional) rower and I can guarantee you that after half an hour of dancing at a club, I can't catch my breath. So, if Taylor Swift, who hasn't been slammed for promoting "unhealthy weight" can barely get through an hour and a half set, and Lizzo, full of jois-de-vivre can, then it's pretty obvious we're actually just being fatphobic.

Not only is weight a false signifier of health, this whole ordeal is really about the burden of representation. Lizzo is probably the only powerful woman in the spotlight who doesn't conform to society's bodily expectations, so the burden of representation lies with her. Because she's different, we attribute everything she does as a "statement." Why do celebrity women have to be promoting some kind of thing? Why is it that if they are doing anything, there's a message behind it?

Lizzo told *Glamour*: "if you saw Anna Hathaway in a bikini on a billboard, you wouldn't call her brave." Hitting the nail on the head, she explained that "a form of protest for fat bodies and black women" has merely become about "going to the spa, getting your nails done or drinking a mimosa." As if, just existing and enjoying life is a "protest" simply because you don't conform to standards.

There's something to be said about the main focus of body positivity "gone wrong" centering on female celebrities. Women send "messages" with their body, while men merely have bodies. Nobody is angrily writing tweets about Jack Black and his promotion of obesity, or James Corden and his "chubby tummy." In fact, when I typed in "fat male celebrities" all that came up was "Successful Fat People" and a Tumblr blog aimed at "appreciating different body types." When I typed in "fat female celebrities" I got "50 Fat Celebrities."

Is this because we live in a world where people believe that shaming individuals somehow makes a problem go away? As if writing scathing comments on Lizzo's Instagram will convince everyone to be aware of diabetes and eating unhealthily? The problem with Lizzo is that people can't believe she has the audacity to be "fat" and the audacity to be proud of her body. It's society's way of regulating people who fall outside of the norm. If anything, we need more Lizzos, more people who are unapologetically themselves, because there's nothing wrong with being who you are.

14

Healthy Eating and Exercising Are Important to Preventing Obesity

Yasmine S. Ali

Yasmine S. Ali, MD, MSCI, is a cardiologist and a physician-writer whose work has appeared in Very Well Health, Nashville Paw Magazine, *and the* Tennessean.

There are several steps one can take to prevent obesity. They include following a plant-based diet, healthy eating, avoiding processed food, and reducing sugar consumption. One of the most important steps to reduce risks of obesity is focusing mostly on eating fruits and vegetables, which help you feel full without the barrage of calories. Those who want to work on preventing obesity should also eliminate artificial sweeteners from their diet as they are linked to a growing risk of obesity and diabetes. Lastly, exercise plays a big role in obesity prevention.

You may be concerned about preventing obesity because of creeping weight gain, a family history of overweight, a related medical concern, or even just an overall concern about staying healthy. Whatever your reason, the goal is a worthy one. Preventing obesity helps you reduce your risk of a host of associated health issues, from heart disease to diabetes to some cancers and much more.

Like many chronic conditions, obesity is preventable with a healthy lifestyle—staying active, following a healthy diet, getting

"How to Prevent Obesity," by Yasmine S. Ali, MD, MSCI, Dotdash Publishing Family, February 13, 2020. Reprinted by permission.

adequate sleep, and so on. The strategies for prevention are also those for treatment if you are already overweight or obese.

More and more research is being directed at obesity prevention. The disease is now a global health epidemic affecting more than 650 million people worldwide, according to the World Health Organization.

Diet

Obesity can be prevented by following basic principles of healthy eating. Here are simple changes you can make to your eating habits that will help you lose weight and prevent obesity.

Eat Five a Day

Focus on eating at least five to seven servings of whole fruits and vegetables every day. Fruits and vegetables constitute low-calorie foods. According to WHO, there is convincing evidence that eating fruits and vegetables decreases the risk of obesity. They contain higher amounts of nutrients and are associated with a lower risk for diabetes and insulin resistance. Their fiber content in particular helps you feel full with fewer calories, helping to prevent weight gain.

Avoid Processed Foods

Highly processed foods, like white bread and many boxed snack foods, are a common source of empty calories, which tend to add up quickly. A 2019 study published in Cell Metabolism found that study subjects who were offered a highly processed diet consumed more calories and gained weight, while those offered a minimally processed diet ate less and lost weight.

Reduce Sugar Consumption

It is important to keep your intake of added sugars low. The American Heart Association recommends that the intake of added sugar not exceed 6 teaspoons daily for women and 9 teaspoons daily for men. Major sources of added sugar to avoid include sugary beverages, including sodas and energy or sports drinks;

grain desserts like pies, cookies, and cakes; fruit drinks (which are seldom 100% fruit juice); candy; and dairy desserts like ice cream.

Limit Artificial Sweeteners

Artificial sweeteners have been linked to obesity and diabetes. If you feel you must use a sweetener, opt for a small amount of honey, which is a natural alternative.

Skip Saturated Fats

A 2018 study published in the journal *Biomedica* shows that eating foods high in saturated fat contributes to obesity. Focus instead on sources of healthy fats (monounsaturated and polyunsaturated fats), like avocados, olive oil, and tree nuts. Even healthy fats are recommended to be limited to 20-35% of daily calories, and people with elevated cholesterol or vascular disease may need an even lower level.

Sip Wisely

Drink more water and eliminate all sugared beverages from your diet. Make water your go-to beverage; unsweetened tea and coffee are fine, too. Avoid energy drinks or sports drinks, which not only contain an overwhelming amount of added sugar, but have been shown (in the case of the former) to pose potential dangers to the cardiovascular system.

Cook at Home

Studies that have looked at the frequency of home meal preparation have found that both men and women who prepared meals at home were less likely to gain weight. They were also less likely to develop type 2 diabetes.

Try a Plant-Based Diet

Eating a plant-based diet has been associated with greater overall health and much lower rates of obesity. To achieve this, fill your plate with whole vegetables and fruits at every meal. For snacks, eat small amounts (1.5 ounces or a small handful) of unsalted nuts such as almonds, cashews, walnuts and pistachios (all associated with heart health). Go easy (or eliminate altogether) protein sources that are heavy in saturated fats, such as red meat and dairy.

Exercise

Most national and international guidelines recommend that the average adult get at least 150 minutes of moderate-intensity physical activity per week. That means at least 30 minutes per day, five days a week.

The best exercise for maintaining a healthy weight is brisk walking, according to a 2015 analysis of data from the Health Surveys from England.

Researchers found individuals who walk at a brisk or fast pace are more likely to have a lower weight, lower body-mass index (BMI), and lower waist circumference compared to individuals doing other activities.

In addition, experts recommend keeping active throughout the day, whether by using a standing desk, taking frequent stretch breaks, or finding ways to work in walking meetings throughout your day.

Relax

Chronic stress raises levels of the stress hormone cortisol and leads to weight gain. It can also result in poor dietary choices, as cortisol and other stress hormones can increase "carb cravings" and make it difficult to exercise good judgment and willpower.

Look into the many healthy ways to beat stress and find what works best for you. Go for a daily walk, engage in regular yoga or tai chi, meditate, listen to music you love, get together with friends, or do whatever else relaxes you and brings you joy.

Studies show having a pet can lower blood pressure and pets, especially dogs, can increase your level of physical activity and can help you stave off weight gain.

Sleep

The role of sleep in overall well-being cannot be overstated. This extends to the goal of preventing obesity, too. The CDC recommends seven or more hours of sleep for adults 18 and over and even more sleep for younger people.

Studies have linked later bedtimes to weight gain over time. One study of nearly 3,500 adolescents who were followed between 1994 and 2009 in the National Longitudinal Study of Adolescent Health found that a "later average bedtime during the workweek, in hours, from adolescence to adulthood was associated with an increase in BMI over time."

In another study, researchers found that late bedtimes, and therefore less nightly sleep, for 4-year-old and 5-year-old children resulted in a greater likelihood of obesity over time. Specifically, the researchers found that the odds of becoming obese were higher for children who slept less than about 9.5 hours per night, as well as for children who went to bed at 9 p.m. or later.

A Word From Verywell

There are several possible contributors to obesity. The fact that the two biggest ones—diet and activity—are ones you can influence is good news. A healthy lifestyle that puts exercise and eating well at its center can also bring myriad other health benefits. And if you already have obesity or overweight, these strategies can also help you lose weight. Although it can be challenging at times, it is a journey well worth taking.

Note, however, that if you have implemented significant lifestyle changes and are still gaining weight or unable to lose weight, it's important to consult a healthcare professional. There may be an underlying medical condition—such as an endocrine disease (Cushing disease or hypothyroidism) or a disease that causes fluid retention (some liver, heart or kidney disease).

15

The Number of Children with Obesity Has Been on a Steady Rise

Centers for Disease Control and Prevention

The Centers for Disease Control and Prevention is the United States' health protection agency. It keeps the country safe in the face of domestic and foreign health threats.

In the last two decades, the United States has seen a rise in the number of children with obesity. Nevertheless, there are steps that parents, guardians, and teachers can take to help those children. They include helping them develop healthy eating habits, limiting their temptations for calorie-rich food, helping them stay active, reducing their sedentary time, and making sure that they are getting the sleep they need. By helping children with obesity reduce their weight, parents ensure their normal growth and development.

In the United States, the number of children with obesity has continued to rise over the past two decades. Obesity in childhood poses immediate and future health risks.

Parents, guardians, and teachers can help children maintain a healthy weight by helping them develop healthy eating habits and limiting calorie-rich temptations. You also want to help children be physically active, have reduced screen time, and get adequate sleep.

The goal for children who are overweight is to reduce the rate of weight gain while allowing normal growth and development.

"Tips to Help Children Maintain a Healthy Weight," US Department of Health and Human Services.

Children should NOT be placed on a weight reduction diet without the consultation of a health care provider.

Develop Healthy Eating Habits

To help children develop healthy eating habits:

- Provide plenty of vegetables, fruits, and whole-grain products.
- Include low-fat or non-fat milk or dairy products, including cheese and yogurt.
- Choose lean meats, poultry, fish, lentils, and beans for protein.
- Encourage your family to drink lots of water.
- Limit sugary drinks.
- Limit consumption of sugar and saturated fat.

Remember that small changes every day can lead to success!

Limit Calorie-Rich Temptations

Reducing the availability of high-fat and high-sugar or salty snacks can help your children develop healthy eating habits. Only allow your children to eat these foods rarely, so that they truly will be treats! Here are examples of easy-to-prepare, low-fat and low-sugar snacks that are 100 calories or less:

- 1 cup carrots, broccoli, or bell peppers with 2 tablespoons hummus.
- A medium apple or banana.
- 1 cup blueberries or grapes.
- One-fourth cup of tuna wrapped in a lettuce leaf.
- A few homemade oven-baked kale chips.

Help Children Stay Active

In addition to being fun for children, regular physical activity has many health benefits, including:

- Strengthening bones.
- Decreasing blood pressure.
- Reducing stress and anxiety.
- Increasing self-esteem.
- Helping with weight management.

Children ages 3 through 5 years should be active throughout the day. Children and adolescents ages 6 through 17 years should be physically active at least 60 minutes each day. Include aerobic activity, which is anything that makes their hearts beat faster. Also include bone-strengthening activities such as running or jumping and muscle-strengthening activities such as climbing or push-ups.

Remember that children imitate adults. Start adding physical activity to your own routine and encourage your child to join you.

Reduce Sedentary Time

Although quiet time for reading and homework is fine, limit the time children watch television, play video games, or surf the web to no more than 2 hours per day. Additionally, the American Academy of Pediatrics does not recommend television viewing for children aged 2 years or younger. Instead, encourage children to find fun activities to do with family members or on their own that simply involve more activity.

Ensure Adequate Sleep

Too little sleep is associated with obesity, partly because inadequate sleep makes us eat more and be less physically active. Children need more sleep than adults, and the amount varies by age. See the recommended amounts of sleep and suggested habits to improve sleep.

16

The Emotional Release Industry Is Picking Up Steam

Leighanne Higgins and Kathy Hamilton

Leighanne Higgins is a lecturer in marketing at Lancaster University. Kathy Hamilton is a reader in marketing at the University of Strathclyde.

The wellness industry is heavy on healthy eating, exercise, and mindfulness, but a less heralded sector—emotional release—is gaining popularity around the world. Societies that have generally discouraged displays of emotion are now capitalizing on opportunities to offer therapeutic release in controlled environments. Rage clubs, wreck rooms, and crying rooms allow people to release emotions they might normally feel ashamed to display and can contribute to emotional wellness.

When Ariana Grande cried on stage recently, following her performance of an emotionally laden song, she later took to Twitter to apologise and thanked her fans for accepting her humaneness. Producing emotional tears is a uniquely human thing and yet, for many, our first reaction to crying is to apologise.

Public displays of crying and emotional release, especially of emotions deemed as unattractive like being upset or angry, remain taboo. This is because there are socially accepted rules that govern the way we feel things. These "feeling rules" guide the types of emotions and feelings deemed appropriate to display at certain times and places.

These rules tell us that is it acceptable to cry at funerals, but not necessarily at pop concerts. Equally, such rules have often stereotyped certain cultures and genders into particular norms. So feeling rules tend to dictate that men must show greater restraint in expressing their emotions publicly.

The pressure of fast-paced, 24/7 societies has created a deficiency of times and places to release emotion. And into this emotional void a marketplace has sprung up to provide people with places where they can safely vent.

Japan is at the forefront of this. The Japanese, often stereotyped as emotionless, have found ways to cater to a growing demand for emotional release. In response to the stresses of everyday life particularly among women, hotels launched so-called Crying Rooms. These made-to-order rooms come complete with weepy movies, a cozy atmosphere and tissues on surplus, with the aim of providing women a time and space where they can privately release their upset and tears, free from society's judgement and gaze.

The Japanese company Ikemeso Danshi is even building a reputation for its cry-therapy services, during which customers watch emotive short films under the guidance of a "tear courier." In a culture where crying in front of others is taboo, the cathartic benefits of group crying brings stress relief and relaxation, leading many Japanese companies to embrace the service as a useful team-building exercise.

But it's not just Japan that has an emotional release industry. Cities around the world have seen the launch of anger rooms that provide a designated and safe space for customers to release rage through destroying objects. The recently launched Rage Club in London is a monthly event marketed as a game where participants "play with different practices to embody, enjoy and express rage." The Wreck Room lets you just smash things up in a room on your own.

For some, these services will represent the unwelcome commercialisation of human interaction and fundamental needs. Others will welcome them as a therapeutic experience.

Judgement-Free Environment

A commonality across these services is that they are an opportunity to release emotions in a judgement-free environment, with like-minded others. These are the key features of our new concept entitled Therapeutic Servicescapes, which outlines how service providers can build an environment where people can healthily release their emotions. Our research was based on a three-year study of the Catholic sanctuary of Lourdes in France. We uncovered three key features that help produce a setting where particular emotions are permitted and released. These features involve:

1) A space that's designed to stimulate particular emotions.
2) Like-minded beliefs provide a sense of safety, security and acceptance of the behaviour and emotions of others.
3) An escape from the dominant cultural feeling rules.

We found that these features catalysed emotional release, which boosted people's emotional well-being. While many of the Japanese services outlined above are aimed at women, our research found the therapeutic environment at Lourdes was crucial to both men and women. Many of the men we spoke to saw it as a safe space, where they could release emotions and cry, free from judgement and stigma. This acceptance of crying, people told us, contrasted with their home cultures that they described as "emotionally straightjacketed."

The value of this kind of service space is evident, especially at a time when society faces a mental health crisis, with men often worse affected by the inability to talk about or release their emotions. Suicide is the number one cause of death for men under 50 in the UK and suicide rates among US men is four times higher than women. Our study shows the importance of creating spaces where men can open up about their feelings, free from the usual societal pressures that stop them from expressing their emotions.

The health and wellness industry is expected to grow to £632 billion globally by 2021, with more and more people spending money on healthy eating, exercise and activities that help their mental health. We see the appeal of services that promote emotional release as a relatively untapped but growing segment of this burgeoning industry.

17

There Are Many Misconceptions Surrounding a Fitness Lifestyle

Paige Waehner

Paige Waehner is a certified personal trainer, fitness writer, and author.

There are a lot of myths surrounding exercising. The most common one is the misconception that there exist specific workouts that can target certain parts of our body for weight loss. Unfortunately, this cannot happen. Through a calorie-deficient diet, regular cardio exercises, and strength training, you can lose weight in various areas of your body. The last place you will lose body fat is where you store excess fat. Oftentimes, it is the belly area.

If you've ever done crunches to get six-pack abs or leg lifts to get thin thighs (and haven't we all?), you've fallen prey to the myth of spot reduction. This myth suggests that doing specific exercises for specific body parts will help you lose body fat there. But, the truth is, how and where we lose fat depends on, among other things, genetics, hormones, and age.

"6 Strength Training Myths Debunked," by Paige Waehner, Dotdash Publishing Family, December 1, 2019. Reprinted by permission.

Myth 1: I Can Reduce Fat Around the Abs or Thighs with Specific Exercises

If you want to lose fat around the thighs or belly, you have to create a calorie deficit (through exercise and diet), lose body fat and see how your body responds. What you'll find is that wherever you store excess fat is that last place you'll lose it. For women, that's often the hips, thighs and lower belly and for men, it's often the belly and waist.

One reason this myth is still hanging around is that of how aggressively it's perpetuated by the infomercials, diets, and magazines promising thin thighs, flat abs and other extreme results for very little work.

Instead of wasting money on false promises and silly gadgets, try a healthier approach so that you can get your best body rather than an idealized body that always seems out of reach:

- Regular cardio exercise in your target heart rate zone
- Strength training for your entire body 1-3 non-consecutive days a week
- A healthy low-calorie diet

A study done by the University of Massachusetts had 13 males do vigorous ab exercises for 27 days, and fat biopsies were taken both before and after the exercise. The results? Subjects decreased fat from different areas of the body, not just the abs.

Myth 2: To Tone My Muscles, I Should Use Lighter Weights and High Reps

This is another myth, what I call "The Pink Dumbbell Myth" that is often perpetuated by magazines and infomercials, convincing us that we should use lighter weights (e.g., pink dumbbells) for higher reps to tone our bodies. There's also a belief that this approach somehow burns more fat and that women should lift weights this way to avoid getting big and bulky.

The truth is that this type of strength training doesn't burn more fat and the only way it will "tone" your body is if you've created a calorie deficit that allows you to lose body fat. Using lighter weights for higher reps will help you increase muscular endurance and it does have a place in training routines, but that lean, defined look comes from losing body fat.

So, does that mean you shouldn't use the lightweight, high-rep approach with strength training? Not necessarily. How you lift weights depends on your goals and fitness level. But, for weight loss, it's great to use a variety of rep and weight ranges.

Choosing Your Reps:

- For strength gains: 1-6 reps, heavy weights
- For gaining muscle and size: 8-12 reps, medium-heavy weights
- For endurance: 12-16 reps (or more), light-medium weights

No matter what range you choose, you should always lift enough weight that you can ONLY complete the desired reps. If you're doing 12 bicep curls, choose a weight that allows you to do 12 reps with good form. If you can do more than that, increase your weight.

Using all three ranges, whether you use them each week, each month or change them every few weeks, is a great way to challenge your body in different ways.

Myth 3: For Fat Burning or Weight Loss, I Should Only Do Cardio Exercise

While cardio is important for burning fat and losing weight, it isn't the only type of exercise that can help you lose fat.

Strength training helps you preserve the muscle you have as well as increase your muscle mass and the more muscle you have, the more calories you'll burn all day long.

Why You Need Strength Training

Remember, muscle is more active than fat. In fact, a pound of muscle can burn anywhere from 10-20 calories a day while a pound of fat burns only 2-5 calories a day. And, don't forget, muscle is more dense than fat and takes up less space. That means when you lose fat and gain muscle, you'll be slimmer and trimmer.

Plenty of people, especially women, avoid strength training like the plague, either because they think they'll gain weight or because they like cardio better. But strength training has a number of benefits such as:

- It builds lean muscle tissue.
- It strengthens muscles, bones and connective tissue.
- It keeps your body strong and injury-free for your cardio workouts.
- It raises metabolism.

An effective fat loss program will include regular strength training and cardio workouts, done either separately or together, depending on your schedule and goals. Another important component is, of course, eating a healthy diet as well. By implementing all three components, you can maximize your weight loss and your health.

Myth 4: I Should Be Sore After Every Workout

How do you know if you've gotten a good strength training workout? A lot of people would measure their workouts by how sore they are the next day, but that isn't the best way to gauge your workout.

Soreness (often called delayed onset muscle soreness or DOMS) is normal if you're a beginner, if you've changed your usual routine or if you're trying new activities. But, that soreness should lessen over time and, if you're sore after every workout, you may need more recovery days or to reduce the intensity of your workouts to allow your body time to adapt and grow stronger.

Soreness is actually caused by small tears in your muscle fibers, which is how muscles respond when overloaded. Rest and recovery are essential for growing stronger and building lean muscle tissue. If you're sore after every workout, you may need more time to recover or you risk overtraining and injury.

How Do You Know if You're Getting a Good Workout?

Lift enough weight. When strength training, you always want to choose a weight heavy enough that you can only complete the desired number of reps. If you stop at the end of a set and realize you could do more, increase your weight so that the last rep is difficult, but not impossible to complete.

Work out all your muscle groups. Whether you do a total body workout or a split routine, make sure you hit all your muscle groups 2-3 times each week, with at least one exercise per muscle group (more if you're more advanced).

Change your program. Make sure you change your routine every 4-6 weeks to avoid plateaus.

To help mitigate soreness, you should warm up before your workout and cool down and stretch the muscles you've used after the workout.

Myth 5: Strength Training Makes Women Big and Bulky

This is another popular myth that persists despite the fact that women typically don't have the number of hormones (namely, testosterone) necessary to build huge muscles. In fact, even men struggle to gain muscle, which is one reason steroids are such a popular drug with men who want to build big muscles.

This myth goes hand in hand with myth #2, convincing women that strength training is for men and that, if they do lift weights, they should stick with the pink dumbbells.

Nothing could be further from the truth.

Why Women Need to Lift Heavy

Lifting heavy weights can benefit both men and women and, in fact, challenging your body with heavy weights is the only way you'll really see results and get stronger. I've been lifting heavy weights for years and have never even come close to looking like a bodybuilder. Most women who lift weights would agree. Remember, muscle takes up less space than fat. When you add muscle, that helps you lose fat (along with your cardio and healthy diet, of course), which means you'll be leaner and more defined.

If you're still reluctant to lift weights because you've never tried and you have no idea where to start, try the Total Body Strength for Beginners workout, which starts you out with the basics of a solid strength program.

Myth 6: I'm Too Old to Lift Weights

Of course, if you have medical issues or conditions you would need to visit the doctor to get clearance but, beyond that, there's no age limit on beginning a strength program and, even better, the improvements you see will make your life better.

The Benefits of Exercise

- Better functioning
- Improved balance and coordination
- Greater strength and flexibility
- Weight management
- More confidence
- Reduced risk of falling down
- Building strong, lean muscle

In fact, the risks associated with not exercising and lifting weights are much greater than a safe, effective strength program. In fact, without exercise, we could lose 3-5% of our muscle mass per decade after age 40, what experts call sarcopenia. This loss of muscle doesn't just cause weight gain, but it also contributes to reduced functionality and strength.

You don't have to spend hours lifting heavy weights to get the benefits, either.

18

Consumer Wearables for Health and Performance Are the Future

Jonathan M. Peake, Graham Kerr, and John P. Sullivan

Jonathan M. Peake and Graham Kerr are affiliated with the Institute of Health and Biomedical Innovation at Queensland University of Technology. John P. Sullivan is an internationally renowned sports scientist, best-selling author, and visiting scholar at the Queensland Academy of Sport.

Devices that measure and evaluate steps, heartrate, sleep, and other personal data have become fairly common, but the wearables industry has much more potential than we are currently seeing. Even in the relatively narrow focus of fitness, technology is continually advancing to allow athletes to measure hydration, metabolism, breathing patterns, cognitive function, and injury risks.

The commercial market for technologies to monitor and improve personal health and sports performance is ever expanding. A wide range of smart watches, bands, garments, and patches with embedded sensors, small portable devices and mobile applications now exist to record and provide users with feedback on many different physical performance variables. These variables include cardiorespiratory function, movement patterns, sweat analysis, tissue oxygenation, sleep, emotional state, and changes in cognitive function following concussion. In this review, we have summarized the features and evaluated the characteristics of a cross-section of technologies for health and sports performance according to what the technology is claimed to do, whether it has been validated and is reliable, and if it is suitable for general consumer use. Consumers who are choosing new technology should consider whether it (1) produces desirable (or non-desirable) outcomes, (2) has been developed based on real-world need, and (3) has been tested and proven effective in applied studies in different settings. Among the technologies included in this review, more than half have not been validated through independent research. Only 5% of the technologies have been formally validated. Around 10% of technologies have been developed for and used in research. The value of such technologies for consumer use is debatable, however, because they may require extra time to set up and interpret the data they produce. Looking to the future, the rapidly expanding market of health and sports performance technology has much to offer consumers. To create a competitive advantage, companies producing health and performance technologies should consult with consumers to identify real-world need, and invest in research to prove the effectiveness of their products. To get the best value, consumers should carefully select such products, not only based on their personal needs, but also according to the strength of supporting evidence and effectiveness of the products.

Introduction

The number and availability of consumer technologies for evaluating physical and psychological health, training emotional awareness, monitoring sleep quality, and assessing cognitive function has increased dramatically in recent years. This technology is at various stages of development: some has been independently tested to determine its reliability and validity, whereas other technology has not been properly tested. Consumer technology is moving beyond basic measurement and telemetry of standard vital signs, and predictive algorithms based on static population-based information. Health and performance technology is now moving toward miniaturized sensors, integrated computing, and artificial intelligence. In this way, technology is becoming "smarter," more personalized with the possibility of providing real-time feedback to users (Sawka and Friedl, 2018). Technology development has typically been driven by bioengineers. However, effective validation of technology for the "real world" and development of effective methods for processing data requires collaboration with mathematicians and physiologists (Sawka and Friedl, 2018).

Although there is some overlap between certain technologies, there are also some differences, strengths and weaknesses between related technologies. Various academic reviews have summarized existing technologies (Duking et al., 2016; Halson et al., 2016; Piwek et al., 2016; Baron et al., 2017). However, the number and diversity of portable devices, wearable sensors and mobile applications is ever increasing and evolving. For this reason, regular technology updates are warranted. In this review, we describe and evaluate emerging technologies that may be of potential benefit for dedicated athletes, so-called "weekend warriors," and others with a general interest in tracking their own health. To undertake this task, we compiled a list of known technologies for monitoring physiology, performance and health, including concussion. Devices for inclusion in the review were identified by searching the internet and databases of scientific literature (e.g., PubMed) using key terms such as "technology," "hydration," "sweat analysis," "heart rate," "respiration," "biofeedback," "respiration," "muscle oxygenation," "sleep," "cognitive function," and "concussion." We examined the websites for commercial technologies for links to research, and where applicable, we sourced published research literature. We broadly divided the technologies into the following categories:

- devices for monitoring hydration status and metabolism
- devices, garments, and mobile applications for monitoring physical and psychological stress

- wearable devices that provide physical biofeedback (e.g., muscle stimulation, haptic feedback)
- devices that provide cognitive feedback and training
- devices and applications for monitoring and promoting sleep
- devices and applications for evaluating concussion.

Our review investigates the key issues of: (a) what the technology is claimed to do; (b) has the technology been independently validated against some accepted standard(s); (c) is the technology reliable and is any calibration needed, and (d) is it commercially available or still under development. Based on this information we have evaluated a range of technologies and provided some unbiased critical comments. The list of products in this review is not exhaustive; it is intended to provide a cross-sectional summary of what is available in different technology categories.

Devices for Monitoring Hydration Status and Metabolism

Several wearable and portable hardware devices have been developed to assess hydration status and metabolism. Very few of the devices have been independently validated to determine their accuracy and reliability. The Moxy device measures oxygen saturation levels in skeletal muscle. The PortaMon device measures oxy-, deoxy-, and total hemoglobin in skeletal muscle. These devices are based on principles of near infrared spectroscopy. The PortaMon device has been validated against phosphorus magnetic resonance spectroscopy (31P-MRS) (Ryan et al., 2013). A similar device (Oxymon) produced by the same company has been proven to produce reliable and reproducible measurements of muscle oxygen consumption both at rest (coefficient of variation 2.4%) and after exercise (coefficient of variation 10%) (Ryan et al., 2012). Another study using the Oxymon device to measure resting cerebral oxygenation reported good reliability in the short term (coefficient of variation 12.5%) and long term (coefficient of variation 15%) (Claassen et al., 2006). The main limitation of these devices is that some expertise is required to interpret the data that they produce. Also, although these devices are based on the same scientific principles, they do vary in terms of the data that they produce (McManus et al., 2018).

The BSX Insight wearable sleeve has been tested independently (Borges and Driller, 2016). Compared with blood lactate measurements during a graded exercise test, this device has high to very high agreement (intraclass correlation coefficient >0.80). It also has very good reliability (intraclass correlation coefficient 0.97; coefficient of variation 1.2%) (Borges and Driller, 2016). This device likely offers some useful features for monitoring muscle oxygenation and lactate non-invasively during exercise. However, one limitation is that the sleeve that houses the device is currently designed only for placement on the calf, and may therefore not be usable for measuring muscle oxygenation in other muscle groups. The Humon Hex is a similar device for monitoring muscle oxygenation that is touted for its benefits in guiding warm-ups, monitoring exercise thresholds and recovery. For these devices, it is unclear how reference limits are set, or established for such functions.

Other non-wearable devices for monitoring metabolism, such as Breezing and the LEVL device, only provide static measurements, and are therefore unlikely to be useful for measuring metabolism in athletes while they exercise. Sweat pads/patches have been developed at academic institutions for measuring skin temperature, pH, electrolytes, glucose, and cortisol (Gao et al., 2016; Koh et al., 2016; Kinnamon et al., 2017). These devices have potential applications for measuring heat stress, dehydration and metabolism in athletes, soldiers, firefighters, and industrial laborers who exercise or work in hot environments. Although these products are not yet commercially available, they likely offer greater validity than existing commercial devices because they have passed through the rigorous academic peer review process for publication. Sweat may be used for more detailed metabolomic profiling, but there are many technical and practical issues to consider before this mode of bioanalysis can be adopted routinely (Hussain et al., 2017).

Technologies for Monitoring Training Loads, Movement Patterns, and Injury Risks

A wide range of small attachable devices, garments, shoe insoles, equipment, and mobile applications have been developed to monitor biomechanical variables and training loads. Among biomechanical sensors, many are based around accelerometer and gyroscope technology. Some of the devices that attach to the body provide basic information about body position, movement velocity, jump height, force, power, work, and rotational movement. This data can be used by biomechanists and ergonomists to evaluate movement patterns, assess musculoskeletal fatigue profiles, identify potential risk factors for injury and adjust techniques while walking, running, jumping, throwing, and lifting. Thus, these devices have application in sporting, military and occupational settings.

Among these devices, the I Measure U device is lightweight, compact and offers the greatest versatility. Other devices and garments provide information about muscle activation and basic training metrics (e.g., steps, speed, distance, cadence, strokes, repetitions etc). The mPower is a pod placed on the skin that measures EMG. It provides a simple, wireless alternative to more complex EMG equipment. Likewise, the Athos garments contain EMG sensors, but the garments have not been properly validated. It is debatable whether the Sensoria and Dynafeed garments offer any more benefits than other devices. The Mettis Trainer insoles (and Arion insoles in development) could provide some useful feedback on running biomechanics in the field. None of these devices have been independently tested to determine their validity or reliability. Until such validity and reliability data become available, these devices should (arguably) be used in combination with more detailed motion-capture video analysis.

Various mobile applications have been developed for recording and analyzing training loads and injury records. These applications include a wide range of metrics that incorporate aspects of both physical and psychological load. The Metrifit application provides users with links to related unpublished research on evaluating training stress. Many of the applications record and analyze similar metrics, so it is difficult to differentiate between them. The choice of one particular application will most likely be dictated by individual preferences. With such a variety of metrics—which are generally recorded indirectly—it is difficult to perform rigorous validation studies on these products. Another limitation of some of these applications is the large amount of data they record and how to make sense of all the data.

Technologies for Monitoring Heart Rate, Heart Rate Variability, and Breathing Patterns

Various devices and mobile applications have been developed for monitoring physiological stress and workloads during exercise. The devices offer some potential advantages and functionality over traditional heart rate monitors to assess demands on the autonomic nervous system and the cardiovascular system during and after exercise. They can therefore be used by athletes, soldiers and workers involved in physically demanding jobs (e.g., firefighters) to monitor physical strain while they exercise/work, and to assess when they have recovered sufficiently.

The OmegaWave offers the advantages that it directly records objective physiological data such as the electrocardiogram (ECG) as a measure of cardiac stress and direct current (DC) potential as a measure of the activity of functional systems in the central nervous system. However, one limitation of the OmegaWave is that some of the data it provides (e.g., energy supply, hormonal function, and detoxification) are not measured directly. Accordingly, the validity and meaningfulness of such data is uncertain.

The Zephyr sensor, E4 wristband and Reign Active Recovery Band offer a range of physiological and biomechanical data, but these devices have not been validated independently. The E4 wristband is also very expensive for what it offers. The Mio SLICE™ wristband integrates heart rate and physical activity data with an algorithm to calculate the user's Personal Activity Intelligence score. Over time, the user can employ this score to evaluate their long-term health status. Although this device itself has not been validated, the Personal Activity Intelligence algorithm has been tested in a clinical study (Nes et al., 2017). The results of this study demonstrated that individuals with a Personal Activity Intelligence score ≥100 had a 17–23% lower risk of death from cardiovascular diseases.

The HELO smart watch measures heart rate, blood pressure, and breathing rate. It also claims to have some more dubious health benefits, none of which are supported by published or peer-reviewed clinical studies. One benefit of the HELO smart watch is that it can be programmed to deliver an emergency message to others if the user is ill or injured.

The Biostrap smart watch measures heart rate. Although it has not obviously been validated, the company provides a link to research opportunities using their products, which suggests confidence in their products and a willingness to engage in research. The Lief patch measures stress levels through heart rate variability (HRV) and breathing rate, and provides haptic feedback to the user in the form of vibrations to adjust their emotional state. The option of real-time feedback without connection to other technology may provide some advantages. If worn continuously, it is uncertain if or how this device (and others) distinguishes between changes in breathing rate and HRV associated with "resting" stress, as opposed to exercise stress (Dupré et al., 2018). But it is probably safe to assume that users will be aware of what they are doing (i.e., resting or exercising) during monitoring periods. Other non-wearable equipment is available for monitoring biosignals relating to autonomic function and breathing patterns. MyCalmBeat is a pulse meter that attaches to a finger to assess and train breathing rate, with the goal of improving emotional control. The CorSense HRV device will be available in the future, and will be tailored for athletes by providing a guide to training readiness and fatigue through measurements of HRV. It is unclear how data from these devices compare with applications such as OmegaWave, which measures ECG directly vs. by photoplethysmography.

A range of garments with integrated biosensor technology have been developed. The Hexoskin garment measures cardiorespiratory function and physical activity levels. It has been independently validated (Villar et al., 2015). The device demonstrates very high agreement with heart rate measured by ECG (intraclass correlation coefficient >0.95; coefficient of variation <0.8%), very high agreement with respiration rate measured by turbine respirometer (intraclass correlation coefficient >0.95; coefficient of variation <1.4%), and moderate to very high agreement with hip motion intensity measured using a separate accelerometer placed on the hip (intraclass correlation coefficient 0.80 to 0.96; coefficient of variation <6.4%). This device therefore offers value for money. Other garments including Athos and DynaFeed appear to perform similar functions and are integrated with smart textiles, but have not been validated.

Technologies for Monitoring and Promoting Better Sleep

Many devices have been designed to monitor and/or promote sleep. Baron et al. (2017) have previously published an excellent review on these devices. Sleep technologies offer benefits for anyone suffering sleep problems arising from chronic disease (e.g., sleep apnea), anxiety, depression, medication, travel/work schedules, and environmental factors (e.g., noise, light, ambient temperature). The gold standard for sleep measurement is polysomnography. However, polysomnography typically requires expensive equipment and technical expertise to set up, and is therefore not appropriate for regular use in a home environment.

The Advanced Brain Monitoring Sleep Profiler and Zmachine Synergy have been approved by the US Food and Drug Administration. Both devices monitor various clinical metrics related to sleep architecture, but both are also quite expensive for consumers to purchase. The disposable sensor pads required to measure encephalogram (EEG) signals add an extra ongoing cost. The Somté PSG device offers the advantage of Bluetooth wireless technology for recording EEG during sleep, without the need for cables.

A large number of wearable devices are available that measure various aspects of sleep. Several of these devices have been validated against gold-standard polysomnography. The UP™ and Fitbit Flex™ devices are wristbands connected to a mobile application. One study reported that compared with polysomnography, the UP device has high sensitivity for detecting sleep (0.97), and low specificity for detecting wake (0.37), whereas it overestimates total sleep time (26.6 ± 35.3 min) and sleep onset latency (5.2 ± 9.6 min), and underestimates wake after sleep onset (31.2 ± 32.3 min) (de Zambotti et al., 2015). Another study reported that measurements obtained using the UP device correlated with total sleep time (r = 0.63) and time in bed (r = 0.79), but did not correlate with measurements of deep sleep, light sleep or sleep efficiency (Gruwez et al., 2017). Several studies have reported similar findings for the Fitbit Flex™ device (Montgomery-Downs et al., 2012; Mantua et al., 2016; Kang et al., 2017). In a validation study of the OURA ring, it was shown to record similar total sleep time, sleep latency onset and wake after sleep onset, and had high sensitivity for detecting sleep (0.96). However, it had lower sensitivity for detecting light sleep (0.65), deep sleep (0.51) and rapid eye movement sleep (0.61), and relatively poor specificity for detecting wake (0.48). It also underestimated deep sleep by about 20 min, and overestimated the rapid eye movement sleep stage of sleep by about 17 min (de Zambotti et al., 2017b). Similar results were recently reported for the Fitbit Charge2™ device (de Zambotti et al., 2017a). These devices therefore offer benefits for monitoring some aspects of sleep, but they also have some technical deficiencies.

Various other devices are available that play soft music or emit light of certain colors to promote sleep or wakefulness. Some similar devices are currently in commercial development. Although devices such as the Withings Aura and REM Sleep Tracker, Re-Timer and AYO have not been independently validated, other scientific research supports the benefits of applying blue light to improve sleep quality (Viola et al., 2008; Gabel et al., 2013; Geerdink et al., 2016). The NightWave Sleep Assistant is appealing based on its relatively low price, whereas the Withings Aura and REM Sleep Tracker records sleep patterns. The Re-Timer device is useful based on its portability.

Some devices also monitor temperature, noise and light in the ambient environment to identify potential impediments to restful sleep. The Beddit3 Sleep Tracker does not require the user to wear any equipment. The ResMed S+ and Circadia devices are entirely non-contact, but it is unclear how they measure sleep and breathing patterns remotely.

Technologies for Monitoring Psychological Stress and Evaluating Cognitive Function

The nexus between physiological and psychological stress is attracting more and more interest. Biofeedback on emotional state can assist in modifying personal appraisal of situations, understanding motivation to perform, and informing emotional development. This technology has application for monitoring the health of people who work under mentally stressful situations such as military combat, medical doctors, emergency service personnel (e.g., police, paramedics, fire fighters) and traffic controllers. Considering the strong connection between physiology and psychology in the context of competitive sport, this technology may also provide new explanations for athletic "underperformance" (Dupré et al., 2018).

Technology such as the SYNC application designed by Sensum measures emotions by combining biometric data from third-party smartwatches/wristbands, medical devices for measuring skin conductance and HR and other equipment (e.g., cameras, microphones) (Dupré et al., 2018). The Spire device is a clip that attaches to clothing to measure breathing rate and provide feedback on emotional state through a mobile application. Although this device has not been formally validated in the scientific literature, it was developed through an extended period of university research.

The Feel wristband monitors emotion and provides real-time coaching about emotional control.

In addition to the mobile applications and devices that record and evaluate psychological stress, various applications and devices have also been developed to measure EEG activity and cognitive function. Much of this technology has been extensively engineered, making it highly functional. Although the technology has not been validated against gold standards, there is support from the broader scientific literature for the benefits of biofeedback technology for reducing stress and anxiety (Brandmeyer and Delorme, 2013). The Muse™ device produced by InterAxon is an independent EEG-biofeedback device itself, but it has also been coupled with other biofeedback devices and mobile applications (e.g., Lowdown Focus, Opti Brain™). The integration of these technologies highlights the central value of measuring EEG and the versatility of the Muse™ device. The NeuroTracker application is based around the concept of multiple object tracking, which was established 30 years ago as a research tool (Pylyshyn and Storm, 1988). NeuroTracker has since been developed as a training tool to improve cognitive functions including attention, working memory, and visual processing speed (Parsons et al., 2016). This technology has potential application for testing and training cognitive function in athletes (Martin et al., 2017) and individuals with concussion (Corbin-Berrigan et al., 2018), and improving biological perception of motion in the elderly (Legault and Faubert, 2012). The NeuroTracker application has not been validated.

In the fields of human factors and ergonomics, there is increasing interest in methods to assess cognitive load. Understanding cognitive load has important implications for concentration, attention, task performance, and safety (Mandrick et al., 2016). The temporal association between neuronal activity and regional cerebral blood flow (so-called "neurovascular coupling") is recognized as fundamental to evaluating cognitive load. This assessment is possible by combining ambulatory functional neuroimaging techniques such as EEG and functional near infrared spectroscopy (fNIRS) (Mandrick et al., 2016). Research exists on cognitive load while walking in healthy young and older adults (Mirelman et al., 2014; Beurskens et al., 2016; Fraser et al., 2016), but there does not appear to be any research to date evaluating cognitive load in athletes. A number of portable devices measure fNIRS, and some also measure EEG and EMG. These integrated platforms for measuring/assessing multiple physiological systems present significant value for various applications. These devices all measure physiological signals directly from the brain and other parts of the body. Research using these devices has demonstrated agreement between measurements obtained from fNIRS vs. the gold standard of functional magnetic resonance imaging (Mehagnoul-Schipper et al., 2002; Huppert et al., 2006; Sato et al., 2013; Moriguchi et al., 2017). These devices require some expertise and specialist training.

Concussion is a common occurrence in sport, combat situations, the workplace, and in vehicular accidents. There is an ever-growing need for simple, valid, reliable, and objective methods to evaluate the severity of concussion, and to monitor recovery. A number of mobile applications and wearable devices have been designed to meet this need. These devices are of potential value for team doctors, physical trainers, individual athletes, and parents of junior athletes.

The King-Devick Test® is a mobile application based on monitoring oculomotor activity, contrast sensitivity, and eye movement to assess concussion. It has been tested extensively in various clinical settings, and proven to be easy to use, reliable, valid, sensitive, and accurate (Galetta et al., 2011; King et al., 2015; Seidman et al., 2015; Walsh et al., 2016). Galetta et al. (2011) examined the value of the King-Devick Test® for assessing concussion in boxers. They discovered that worsening scores for the King-Devick Test® were restricted to boxers with head trauma. These scores also correlated ($\rho = 90$; $p = 0.0001$) with scores from the Military Acute Concussion Evaluation, and showed high test–retest reliability (intraclass correlation coefficient 0.97

[95% confidence interval 0.90–1.0]). Other studies have reported a very similar level of reliability (King et al., 2015). Performance in the King-Devick Test® is significantly impaired in American football players (Seidman et al., 2015), rugby league players (King et al., 2015), and combat soldiers (Walsh et al., 2016) experiencing concussion. Because the King-Devick Test® is simple to use, it does not require any medical training, and is therefore suitable for use in the field by anyone.

The EyeSync® device employs a simple test that records eye movement during a 15-s circular visual stimulus, and provides data on prediction variability within 60 s. It is not yet commercially available, and has therefore not been validated. The BrainCheck Sport™ mobile application employs the Flanker and Stroop Interference test to assess reaction time, the Digit Symbol Substitution test to evaluate general cognitive performance, the Trail Making test to measure visual attention and task switching, and the Coordination test. It has not been independently validated, but is quick and uses an array of common cognitive assessment tools.

The Sway mobile application tests balance and reaction. Its balance measurements have been validated in small scale studies (Patterson et al., 2014a,b). Performance in the Sway test was inversely correlated ($r = -0.77$; $p < 0.01$) with performance in the Balance Error Scoring System test (Patterson et al., 2014a) and positively correlated ($r = 0.63$; $p < 0.01$) with performance in the Biodex Balance System SD (Patterson et al., 2014b). Further testing is needed to confirm these results. One limitation of this test is the risk of bias that may occur if individuals intentionally underperform during baseline testing to create lower scores than they may attain following a concussion (so as to avoid time out of competition after concussion). Various microsensors have been developed for measuring impact forces associated with concussion. Some of these microsensors attach to the skin, whereas others are built into helmets, headwear or mouth guards. The X-Patch Pro device is a device that attaches behind the ear. Although it has not been scientifically validated against any gold standard, it has been used in published concussion research projects (Swartz et al., 2015; Reynolds et al., 2016), which supports its sensitivity for assessing head impact forces. The Prevent™ mouth guard is a new device for measuring the impact of head collisions. Its benefits include objective and quantitative data on the external force applied to the head. Many of the sensors vary in accuracy, and only record linear and rotational acceleration. Whereas, many sports involve constantly changing of direction, planes of movement will provide the most accurate data. A study by Siegmund et al. (2016) reported that the Head Impact Telemetry System (HITS) sensors detected 861 out of the 896 impacts (96.1%). If a sensor is detecting better than 95%, it has good reliability. However, helmetless sports have fewer options for such accuracy and actionable data.

Considerations and Recommendations

In a brief, yet thought-provoking commentary on mobile applications and wearable devices for monitoring sleep, Van den Bulck makes some salient observations and remarks that are applicable to all forms of consumer health technologies (Van den Bulck, 2015). Most of these technologies are not labeled as medical devices, yet they do convey explicit or implicit value statements about our standard of health. There is a need to determine if and how using technology influences peoples' knowledge and attitude about their own health. The ever-expanding public interest in health technologies raises several ethical issues (Van den Bulck, 2015). First, self-diagnosis based on self-gathered data could be inconsistent with clinical diagnoses provided by medical professionals. Second, although self-monitoring may reveal undiagnosed health problems, such monitoring on a large population level is likely to result in many false positives. Last, the use of technologies may create an unhealthy (or even harmful) obsession with personal health for individuals or their family members who use such technologies (Van den Bulck, 2015). Increasing public awareness of the limitations of technology and advocating health technologies that are both specific and sensitive to certain aspects of health may alleviate these issues to some extent, but not entirely.

For consumers who want to evaluate technologies for health and performance, we propose a matrix based around two dimensions: strength of evidence (weak to strong) and effectiveness (low to high). This matrix is based on a continuum that was developed for use in a different context (Puddy and Wilkins, 2011), but is nonetheless appropriate for evaluating technology. When assessing the strength of evidence for any given technology, consumers should consider the following questions: (i) how rigorously has the device/technology been evaluated? (ii) how strong is the evidence in determining that the device/technology is producing the desired outcomes? (iii) how much evidence exists to determine that something other than this device/technology is responsible for producing the desired outcomes? When evaluating the effectiveness of technologies, consumers should consider whether the device/technology produces desirable or non-desirable outcomes. Applying the matrix, undetermined technologies would include those that have not been developed according to any real-world need and display no proven effect. Conversely, well-supported technologies would include those that have been used in applied studies in different settings, and proven to be effective.

Most of the health and performance technologies that we have reviewed have been developed based on real-world needs, yet only a small proportion has been proven effective through rigorous, independent validation. Many of these technologies described in this review should therefore be classified "emerging" or "promising." Independent scientific validation provides the strongest level of support for technology. However, it is not always possible to attain higher standards of validation. For example, cognitive function is underpinned by many different neurological processes. Accordingly, it is difficult to select a single neurological measurement to compare against. Some technologies included in this review have not been independently validated per se; but through regular use in academic research, it has become accepted that they provide reliable and specific data on measurement items of interest. Even without formal independent validation, it is unlikely (in most instances at least) that researchers would continue using such technologies if they did not offer reliable and specific data. In the absence of independent validation, we therefore propose that technologies that have not been validated against a gold standard (but are regularly used in research) should be considered as "well-supported." Other technical factors for users to consider include whether the devices require calibration or specialist training to set up and interpret data, the portability and physical range for signal transmission/recording, Bluetooth/ ANT+ and real-time data transfer capabilities, and on-board or cloud data storage capacity and security.

From a research perspective, consumer health technologies can be categorized into those that have been used in validation studies, observational studies, screening of health disorders, and intervention studies (Baron et al., 2017). For effective screening of health disorders and to detect genuine changes in health outcomes after lifestyle interventions, it is critical that consumer health technologies provide valid, accurate and reliable data (Van den Bulck, 2015). Another key issue for research into consumer health technologies is the specificity of study populations with respect to the intended use of the technologies. If technologies have been designed to monitor particular health conditions (e.g., insomnia), then it is important for studies to include individuals from the target population (as well as healthy individuals for comparison). Scientific validation may be more achievable in healthy populations compared with populations who have certain health conditions (Baron et al., 2017). There is some potential value for commercial technology companies to create registries of people who use their devices. This approach would assist in collecting large amounts of data, which would in turn provide companies with helpful information about the frequency and setting (e.g., home vs. clinic) of device use, the typical demographics of regular users, and possible feedback from users about devices. Currently, very few companies have established such registries, and they are not consistently publishing data in scientific journals. Proprietary algorithms used for data processing, the lack of access to data by independent scientists, and non-random assignment of device use are also factors that are restricting open engagement between the technology industry and the public at the present time (Baron et al., 2017).

It would seem advisable for companies producing health and performance technologies to consult with consumers to identify real-world needs and to invest in research to prove the effectiveness of their products. However, this seems to be relatively rare. Budget constraints may prevent some companies from engaging in research. Alternatively, some companies may not want to have their products tested independently out of a desire to avoid public scrutiny about their validity. In the absence of rigorous testing, before purchasing health and performance technologies, consumers should carefully consider whether such technologies are likely to be genuinely useful and effective.

Organizations to Contact

The editors have compiled the following list of organizations concerned with the issues debated in this book. The descriptions are derived from materials provided by the organizations. All have publications or information available for interested readers. The list was compiled on the date of publication of the present volume; the information provided here may change. Be aware that many organizations take several weeks or longer to respond to inquiries, so allow as much time as possible.

Be Real Campaign

YMCA England & Wales
10-11 Charterhouse Square
London EC1M 6EH
England
email: bereal@ymca.org.uk
website: berealcampaign.co.uk

The Be Real Campaign is part of the YMCA chapter in England. Its purpose is to promote body confidence in children and adults alike by focusing on three areas: real education, real health, and real diversity.

The Body Positive

PO Box 7801
Berkeley, CA 94707
email: info@thebodypositive.org
website: thebodypositive.org

The Body Positive is an organization founded in 1996 to advocate against the way society creates a self-conscious culture. It celebrates all body types and teaches people to love themselves.

Business Group on Health
20 F Street NW, Suite 200
Washington, DC 20001-6705
(202) 558-3000
email: info@businessgrouphealth.org
website: businessgrouphealth.org

This organization provides tools to employers as they provide health care benefits and wellness resources to their employees. Helping organizations create wellness in workforce strategy is part of the support it provides.

The Cybersmile Foundation
530 Lytton Avenue, 2nd Floor
Palo Alto, CA 94301
email: info@cybersmile.org
website: cybersmile.org

The Cybersmile Foundation focuses on a different kind of wellness: digital well-being. It does so by focusing on creating a more inclusive and kinder digital community.

Global Wellness Institute
333 S.E. 2nd Avenue, Suite 2048
Miami, FL 33131
(212) 716-1199
email: beatrice.hochegger@globalwellnessinstitute.org
website: globalwellnessinstitute.org

The Global Wellness Institute provides the research necessary to educate people about preventative wellness practices. Its website wellnessevidence.com serves as a resource center for health care professionals and others to find research-based evidence on practices like chiropractic.

HERO

24 South Olive Street, Suite 301
Waconia, MN 55387
(952) 835-4257
email: info@hero-health.org
website: hero-health.org

HERO champions a healthy workplace. Organizations are able to become members. It helps in establishing healthy work environments by providing networking, research, education, and engagement opportunities.

National Organization for Women

(202) 570-4745
email: press@now.org
website: now.org

The National Organization for Women focuses on equality and justice for women. It is also responsible for the Love Your Body campaign, which fights the negative influence the media has on female body image and promotes body positivity.

National Wellness Institute

PO Box 827
Stevens Point, WI 54481
(715) 342-2969
email: nwi@nationalwellness.org
website: nationalwellness.org

The National Wellness Institute serves as a global networking organization for professionals and students in the health care and wellness fields. It provides professional development opportunities through events, courses, and certifications. By joining NWI chapters on campus, students are able to find support for their career goals.

Obesity Action Coalition

4511 North Himes Avenue, Suite 250
Tampa, FL 33614
(800) 717-3117
email form: https://www.obesityaction.org/our-purpose/contact-us/
website: obesityaction.org
The Obesity Action Coalition supports those affected by obesity through advocacy, education, and support. Among its goals, this organization helps fight bias and discrimination against obesity.

#WeAllGrow Latina Network

email: gabriela@weallgrowlatina.com
website: weallgrowlatina.com

#WeAllGrow Latina was founded in 2010 by entrepreneur Anna Flores. It not only serves as a networking station for Latina influencers, but it also promotes togetherness and well-being in the community.

Wellness Council of America

17002 Marcy Street, Suite 140
Omaha, NE 68118
(402) 827-3590
email: wellworkplace@welcoa.org
website: welcoa.org

The Wellness Council of America's mission is to create healthier American workplaces. To do so, it provides training tools and resources to corporations that are also members of its organization.

Bibliography

Books

Carrie Arnold. *Decoding Anorexia: How Breakthroughs in Science Offer Hope for Eating Disorders.* London, UK: Routledge, 2012.

Jennifer Ashton. *The Self-Care Solution: A Year of Becoming Happier, Healthier, and Fitter—One Month at a Time.* New York, NY: William Morrow, 2019.

Josh Axe. *Keto Diet: Your 30-Day Plan to Lose Weight, Balance Hormones, Boost Brain Health, and Reverse Disease.* New York, NY: Little, Brown Spark, 2019.

Lindo Bacon and Lucy Aphramor. *Body Respect: What Conventional Health Books Get Wrong, Leave Out, and Just Plain Fail to Understand About Weight.* Dallas, TX: BenBella Books, 2014.

Susan Burton. *Empty: A Memoir.* New York, NY: Random House, 2020.

Megan Jayne Crabbe. *Body Positive Power: Because Life Is Already Happening and You Don't Need Flat Abs to Live It.* New York, NY: Basic Books, 2018.

Raymond J. Cronise and Julieanna Hever. *The Healthspan Solution: How and What to Eat to Add Life to Your Years.* New York, NY: Alpha, 2019.

Glennon Doyle. *Untamed.* New York, NY: The Dial Press, 2020.

Barbara Ehrenreich. *Natural Causes: An Epidemic of Wellness, the Certainty of Dying, and Killing Ourselves to Live Longer.* New York, NY: Twelve, 2018.

Jason Fung. *The Obesity Code: Unlocking the Secrets of Weight Loss.* Vancouver, BC: Greystone Books, 2016.

Michael Greger. *How Not to Diet: The Groundbreaking Science of Healthy, Permanent Weight Loss*. New York, NY: Flatiron Books, 2019.

Sofie Hagen. *Happy Fat: Taking Up Space in a World That Wants to Shrink You*. New York, NY: Fourth Estate, 2020.

Renee McGregor. *Orthorexia: When Healthy Eating Goes Bad*. London, UK: Nourish, 2017.

Lauren Muhlheim. *When Your Teen Has an Eating Disorder: Practical Strategies to Help Your Teen Recover from Anorexia, Bulimia, and Binge Eating*. Oakland, CA: New Harbinger Publications, 2018.

Mungi Ngomane. *Everyday Ubuntu: Living Better Together, the African Way*. New York, NY: Harper Design, 2020.

Catherine Price. *Vitamania: How Vitamins Revolutionized the Way We Think About Food*. New York, NY: Penguin Books, 2016.

Hakim Saboowala. *What Is Orthorexia Nervosa? What One Should Know About Orthorexia*. Seattle, WA: Amazon.com Services LLC, 2020.

Cassie Sobelton. *The Employee Wellbeing Handbook: A Guide for Collaboration Across All Departments, Benefit Vendors, and Health Practitioners to Build a Culture of Wellness Within Any Organization*. Venice, FL: Archangel Ink, 2019.

Periodicals and Internet Sources

Renee Cherry, "Well for Culture Is Giving Indigenous Wellness Practices the Recognition They Deserve," *Shape*, October 5, 2020. https://www.shape.com/lifestyle/mind-and-body /well-for-culture-indigenous-wellness

Joe Deacon, "Black Mental Health, Collective Trauma Among Topics for Virtual Wellness Event," WGLT, January 6, 2021.

https://www.wglt.org/post/black-mental-health-collective
-trauma-among-topics-virtual-wellness-event#stream/0

Mitchell Demeter, "Creating a Culture of Mental Wellness in Turbulent Times," *Forbes*, September 22, 2020. https://www
.forbes.com/sites/forbesbusinesscouncil/2020/09/22
/creating-a-culture-of-mental-wellness-in-turbulent
-times/?sh=3381beee6a22

Nicole Dunn, "Four Ways to Create Well-Rounded Corporate Wellness Culture," *Forbes*, April 28, 2020. https://www
.forbes.com/sites/forbesbusinesscouncil/2020/04/28
/four-ways-to-create-well-rounded-corporate-wellness
-culture/?sh=3694c5b3821a

Maya Feller, "Nutritionist Maya Feller: 5 Ways to Diversify the Wellness Industry," NBC News, June 24, 2020. https://www
.nbcnews.com/know-your-value/feature/nutritionist-maya
-feller-5-ways-diversify-wellness-industry-ncna1232046

Evangeline Gallagher, "The Worst Answer to Climate Anxiety: Wellness," *New Republic*, July 29, 2020. https://newrepublic
.com/article/158621/worst-answer-climate-anxiety-wellness

Kelly Gonsalves, "Wellness Doesn't Belong to White Women," The Cut, August 11, 2020. https://www.thecut.com/article
/wellness-doesnt-belong-to-white-women.html

Jessica Knoll, "Smash the Wellness Industry," *New York Times*, June 8, 2019. https://www.nytimes.com/2019/06/08
/opinion/sunday/women-dieting-wellness.html

Carolyn Kylstra, "Our Definition of Wellness Is Way Too Narrow. It's Time to Change That," *Self*, January 5, 2021.
https://www.self.com/story/redefining-wellness-editor-letter

Brooke Marine, "Fran Lebowitz's Guide to Anti-Wellness," *W*
magazine, January 7, 2021. https://www.wmagazine
.com/story/fran-lebowitz-pretend-its-a-city-docuseries
-interview/

Sophie Mcbain, "The Dark Side of the Wellness Industry," *New Statesman*, June 17, 2020. https://www.newstatesman.com/politics/health/2020/06/dark-side-wellness-industry

Billy McEntee, "Jungle NYC, the New Plant Shop Making Wellness 'Accessible,'" Greenpointers, January 8, 2021. https://greenpointers.com/2021/01/08/jungle-nyc-the-new-plant-shop-making-wellness-accessible/

Brittney McNamara, "Lee from America's Fall from Wellness: What Happens When Wellness Goes Too Far," *Teen Vogue*, January 27, 2020. https://www.teenvogue.com/story/lee-from-america-wellness-goes-too-far

Jenny Singer, "Wellness Drinks Offer Some of the Benefits of Meditation—in a Can," *Glamour*, January 6, 2021. https://www.glamour.com/story/wellness-drinks-offer-meditation-in-a-can

Jessica Thiefels, "What You Need to Know About Workplace Wellness as a Leader," Ladders, December 14, 2020. https://www.theladders.com/career-advice/what-you-need-to-know-about-workplace-wellness-as-a-leader

Index

A

Age Discrimination in
Employment Act, 28
Ali, Mary, 77–80
Ali, Yasmine S., 81–85
Americans with Disabilities
Act, 28
anorexia nervosa, 8
anthrosophy/anthrosophical
medicine, 15
Ao, Bethany, 8
Ardell, Don, 15–16, 17
Ayurveda, 13

B

Berkeley Wellness Letter, 16
Bhutan, and Gross National
Happiness, 19
Bilz, Freidrich, 70
Bircher-Benner, Maximilian, 15
Blanding, Michael, 9
Blei, Daniela, 67–72
body image, 8, 51, 56, 67, 77
body positivity, 10, 77, 80

C

Campbell, Mary, 71
cancer, 26, 45, 81
Carmona, Richard H., 20

Centers for Disease Control
and Prevention, 73, 74,
86–88
chiropractic, 14, 15
Chopra, Deepak, 18
Christian Science, 14, 15
Corte, Ryan, 7

D

diabetes, 9, 19, 26, 30, 32, 33,
42, 48, 51, 77, 78, 80, 81,
82, 83
Dickey, Tom, 16
Dunn, Halbert L., 15, 17, 68,
71, 72

E

eating disorders, 8, 10, 56, 61,
63–66
Eddy, Mary Baker, 15
emotional release industry,
89–92
emotional wellness, 7, 10, 45,
46, 47
environmental wellness, 7, 46
European Wellness Union, 16
exercise/fitness, 7, 8, 10, 13, 14,
15, 35, 37, 40, 43, 46, 51, 54,
60, 69, 70, 71, 72, 74, 81–85,
89, 92, 93–98, 99–116

W

Y